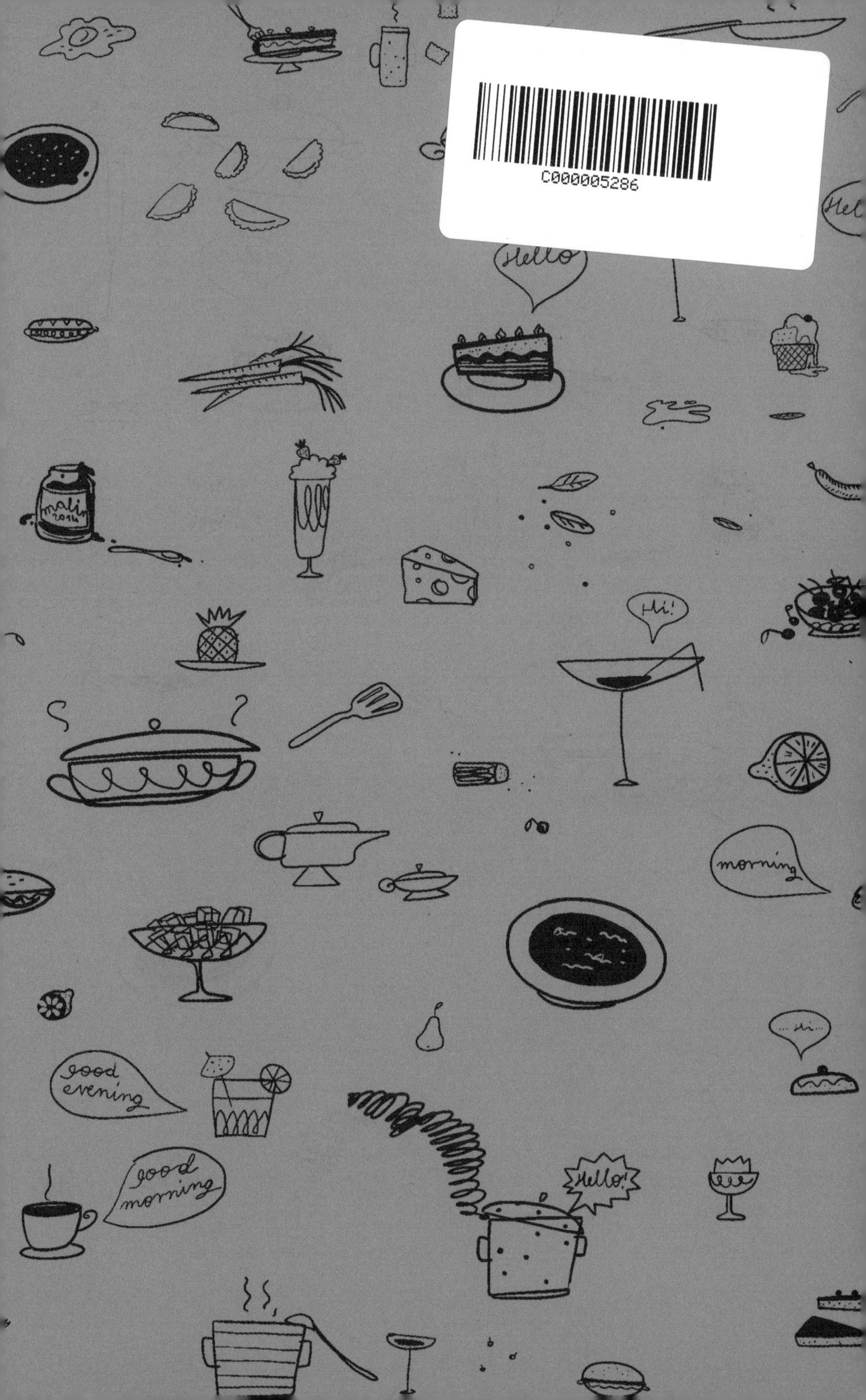
Hello
Hi!
morning
good evening
good morning
Hello!
... hi ...

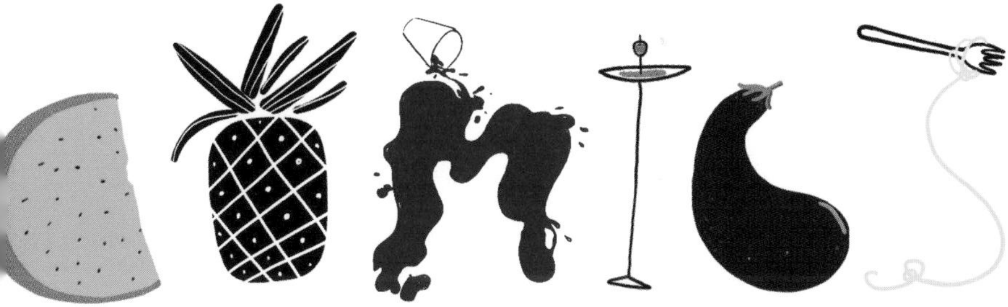
COMICS

# cookbook

First published in Great Britain 2015 by Centrala Ltd
27B Khama Road
London SW17 OEN
www.centrala.org.uk

Copyright © 2015 Centrala Ltd & All Authors
Editorial & Publishing Director: Anna Suska
Special thanks: Ewa Lipińska, Hubert Brychczyński
Cover by Ola Szmida
DTP: gabinet.co.uk

A CIP record for this book is avalable from the British Library

Printed and bound in Poland

ISBN: 978-0-9929082-9-4

Order from www.centrala.org.uk

cookbook

London 2015

centrala
every book matters

PATRONAGE:

SUPPORT:

Smak
Magazyn wokół stołu

# appetisers

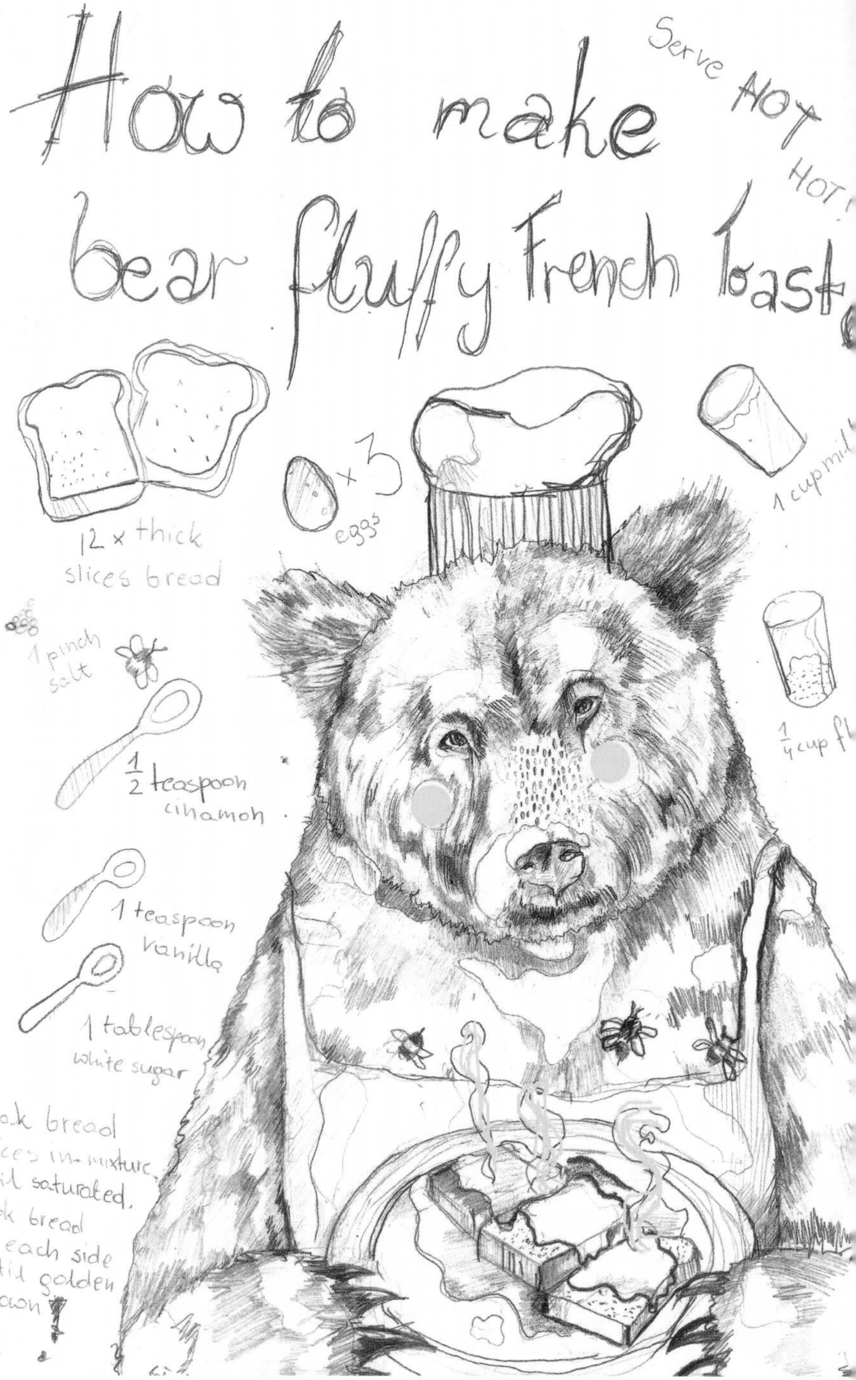
How to make bear fluffy French Toast
Serve HOT HOT
12 x thick slices bread
x 3 eggs
1 cup mil
1 pinch salt
1/2 teaspoon cinamon
1/4 cup f
1 teaspoon vanilla
1 tablespoon white sugar
Soak bread slices in mixture until saturated. Cook bread on each side until golden brown!

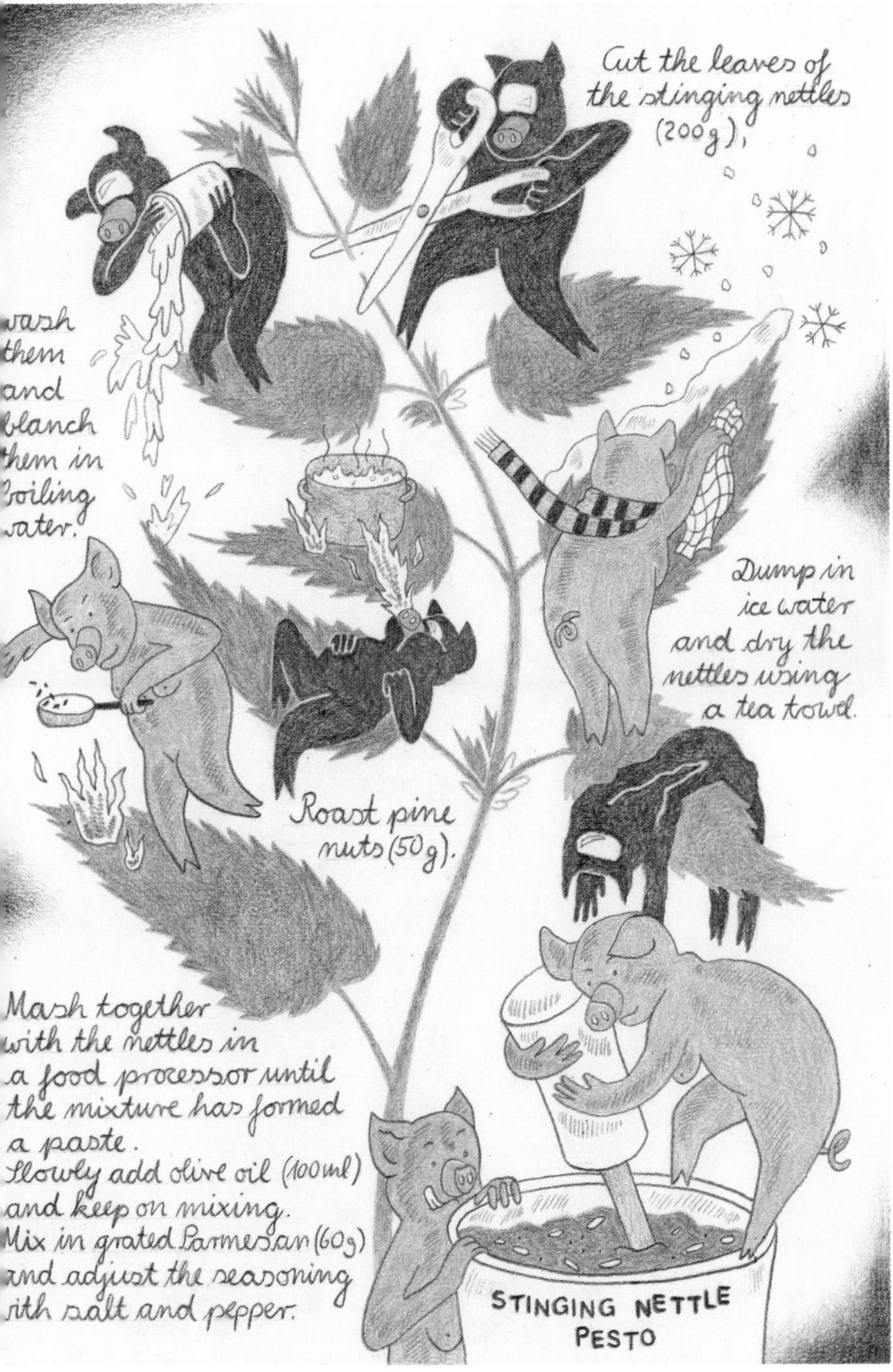
Cut the leaves of the stinging nettles (200g),
vash them and blanch them in boiling water.
Dump in ice water and dry the nettles using a tea towel.
Roast pine nuts (50g).
Mash together with the nettles in a food processor until the mixture has formed a paste.
Slowly add olive oil (100ml) and keep on mixing.
Mix in grated Parmesan (60g) and adjust the seasoning with salt and pepper.
STINGING NETTLE PESTO

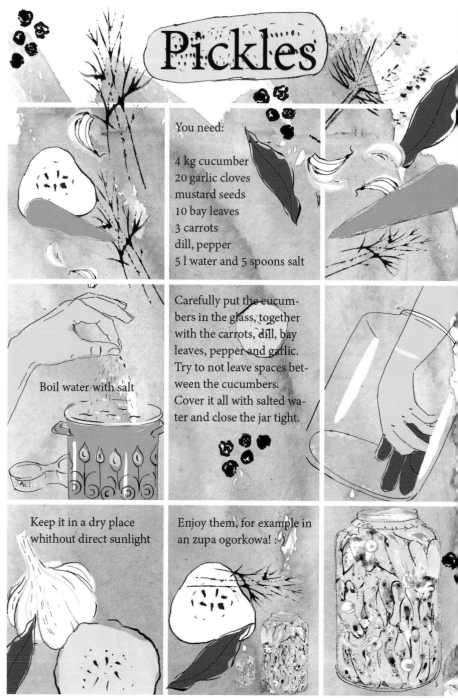

# Pickles

You need:

4 kg cucumber
20 garlic cloves
mustard seeds
10 bay leaves
3 carrots
dill, pepper
5 l water and 5 spoons salt

Boil water with salt

Carefully put the cucumbers in the glass, together with the carrots, dill, bay leaves, pepper and garlic. Try to not leave spaces between the cucumbers. Cover it all with salted water and close the jar tight.

Keep it in a dry place whithout direct sunlight

Enjoy them, for example in an zupa ogorkowa! :-)

8

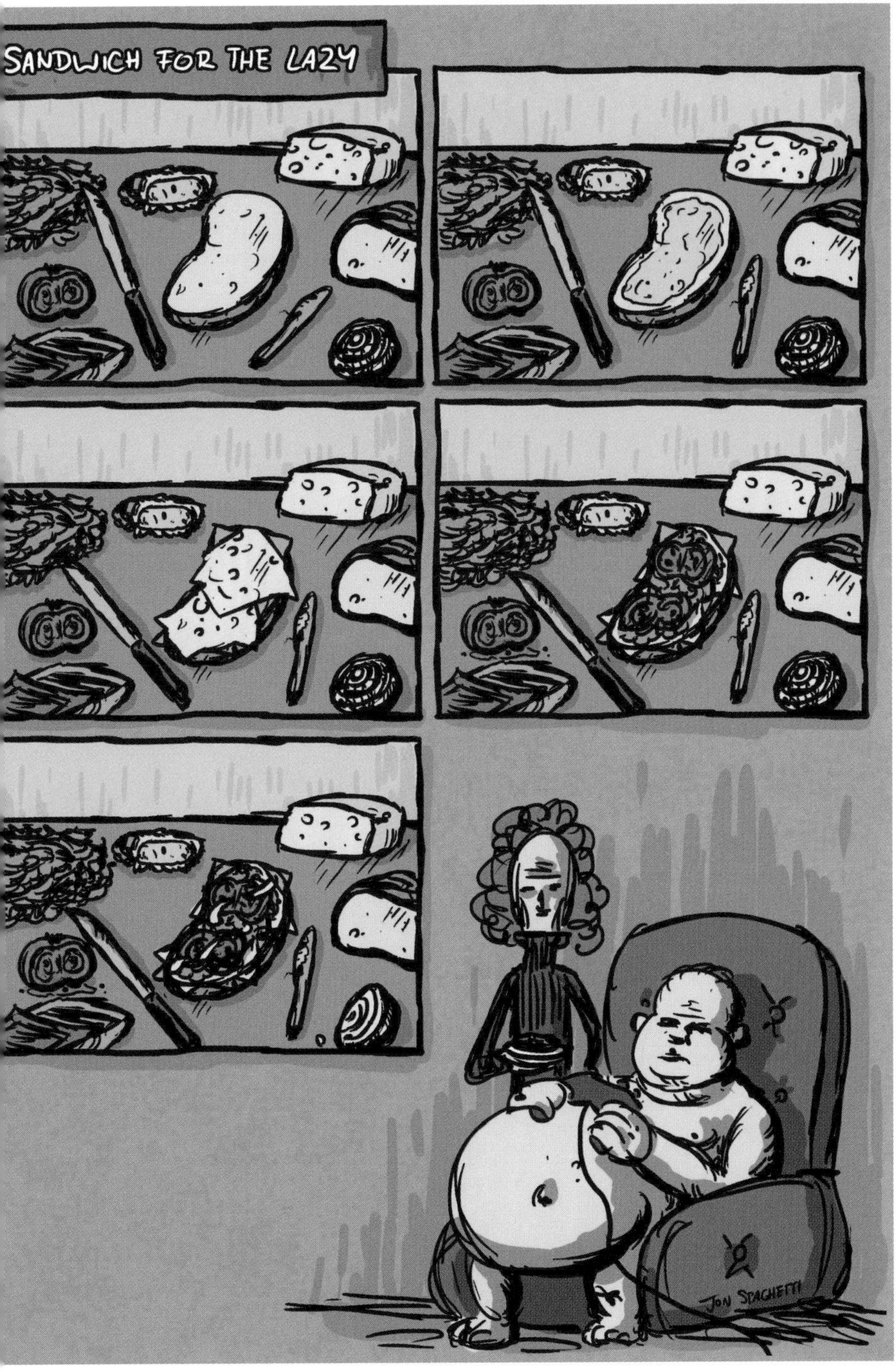
SANDWICH FOR THE LAZY
JON SPAGHETTI

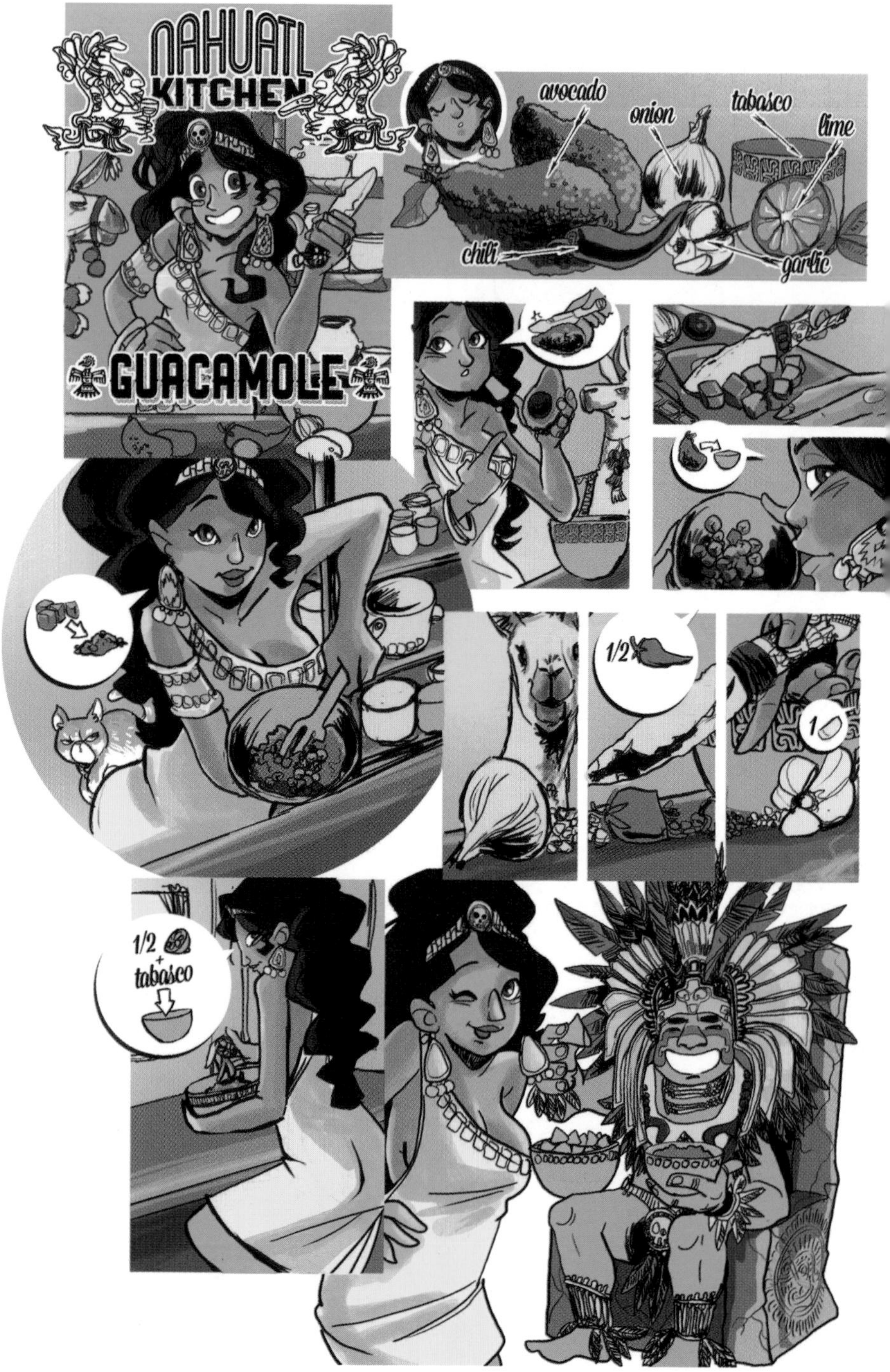
NAHUATL
KITCHEN
GUACAMOLE
avocado
onion
tabasco
lime
chili
garlic
1/2
1/
1/2
+
tabasco

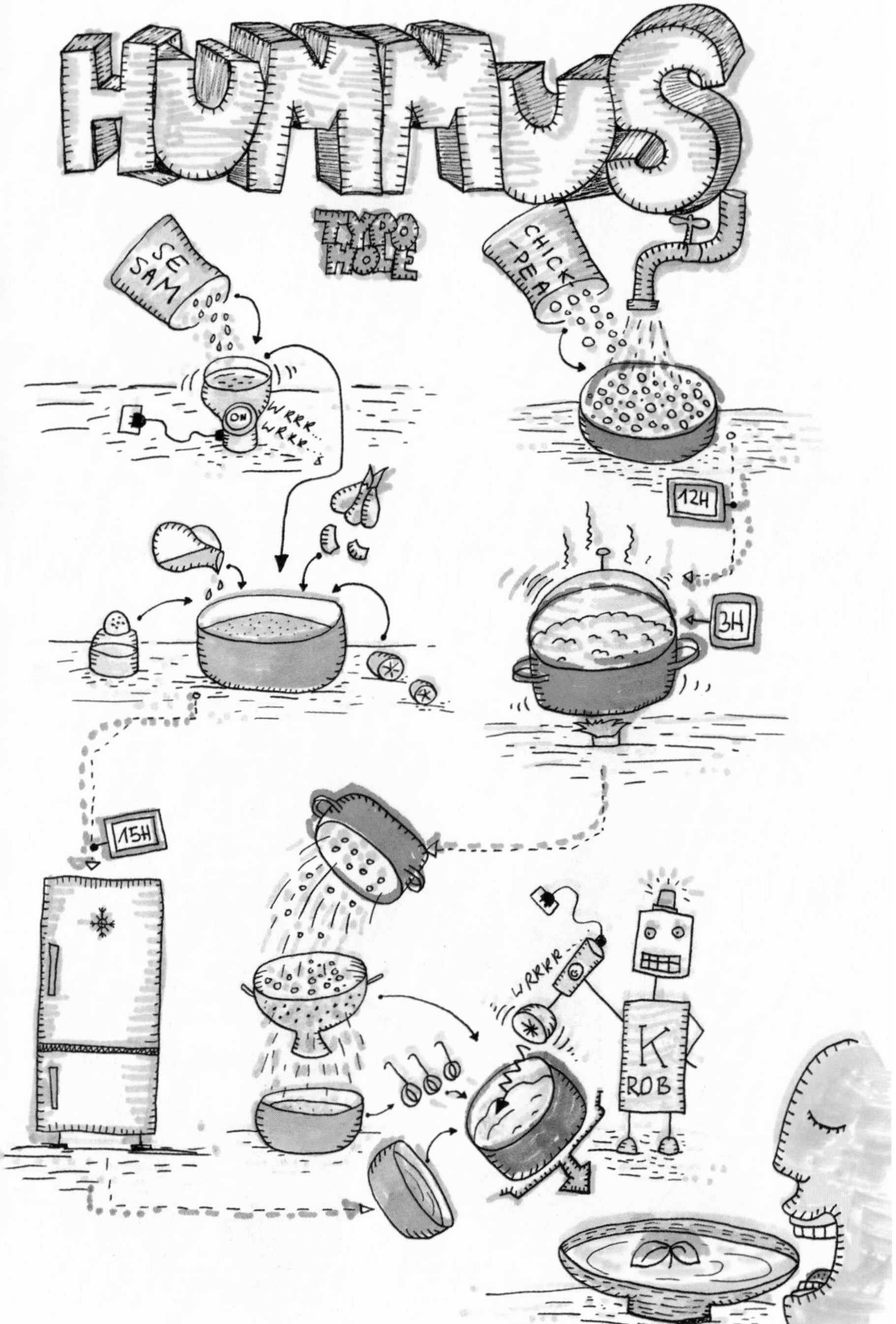
HUMMUS
TYPO HOLE
SE SAM
CHICK -PEA
ON
WRRR... WRRR...
12H
3H
15H
WRRRR
K ROB

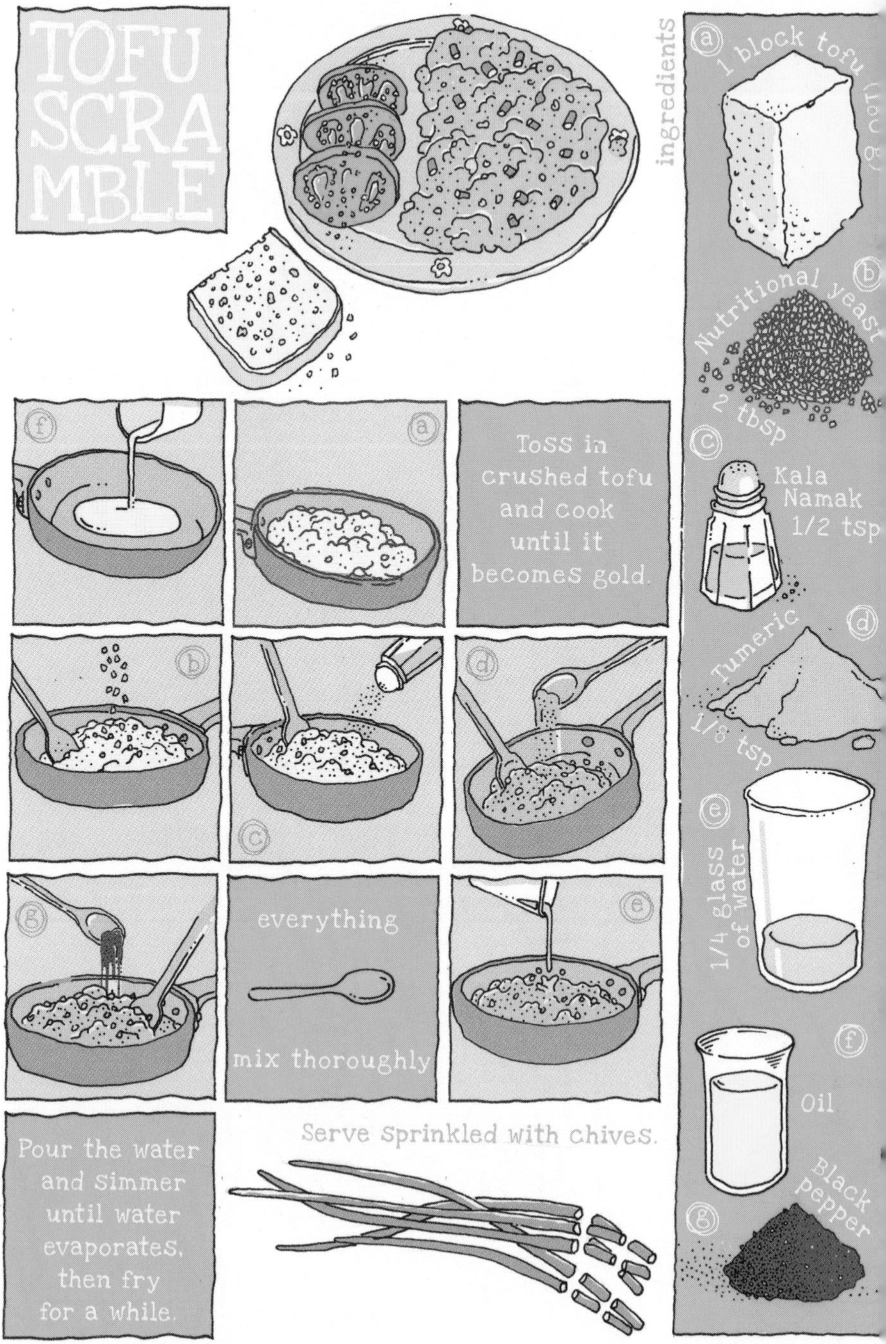
TOFU SCRAMBLE
ingredients
a 1 block tofu
b Nutritional yeast 2 tbsp
c Kala Namak 1/2 tsp
d Tumeric 1/8 tsp
e 1/4 glass of water
f Oil
g Black pepper
f
a
Toss in crushed tofu and cook until it becomes gold.
b
c
d
g
everything
mix thoroughly
e
Pour the water and simmer until water evaporates, then fry for a while.
Serve sprinkled with chives.

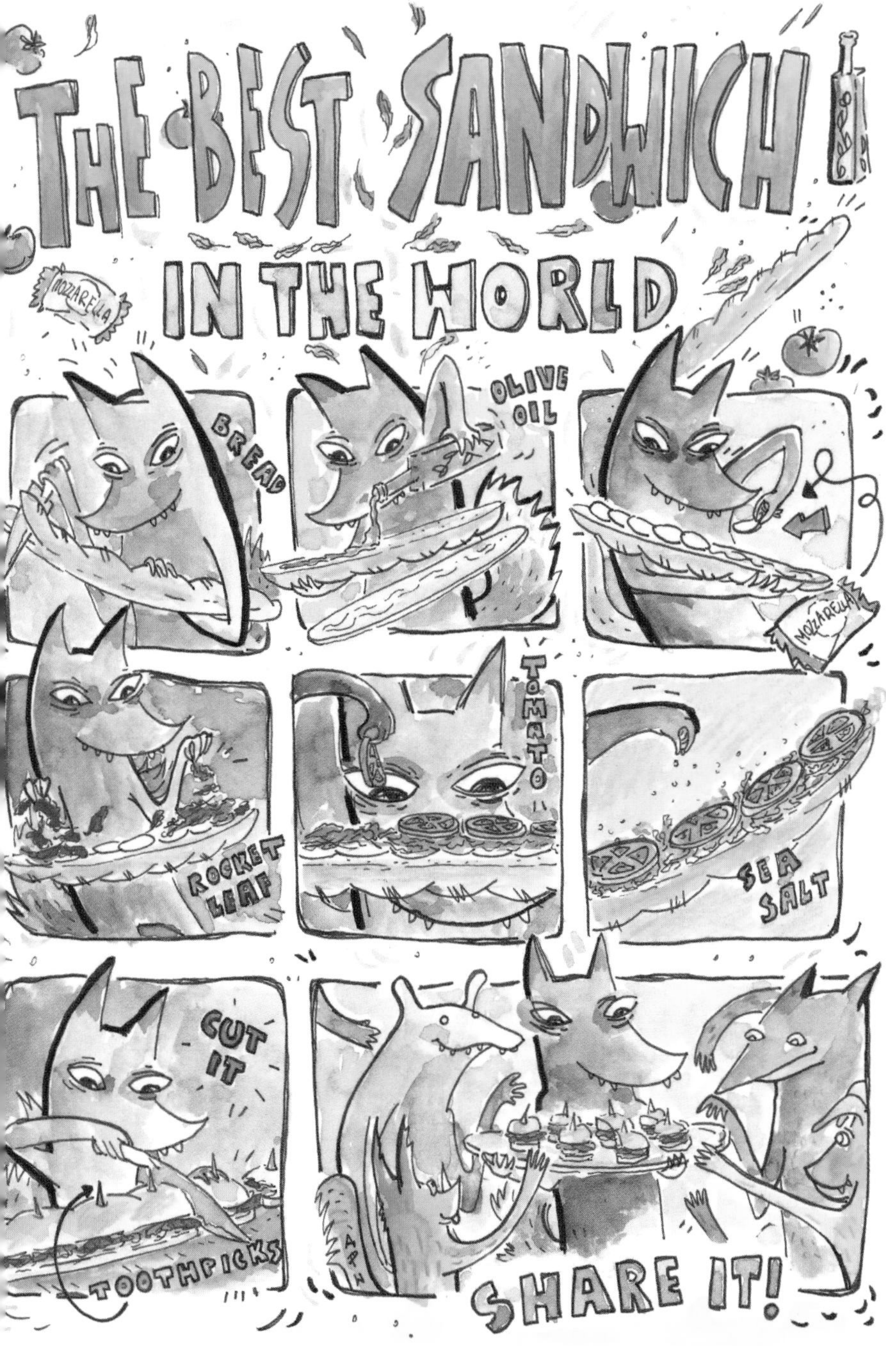
THE BEST SANDWICH
IN THE WORLD
MOZZARELLA
BREAD
OLIVE OIL
MOZZARELLA
TOMATO
ROCKET LEAF
SEA SALT
CUT IT
TOOTHPICKS
SHARE IT!

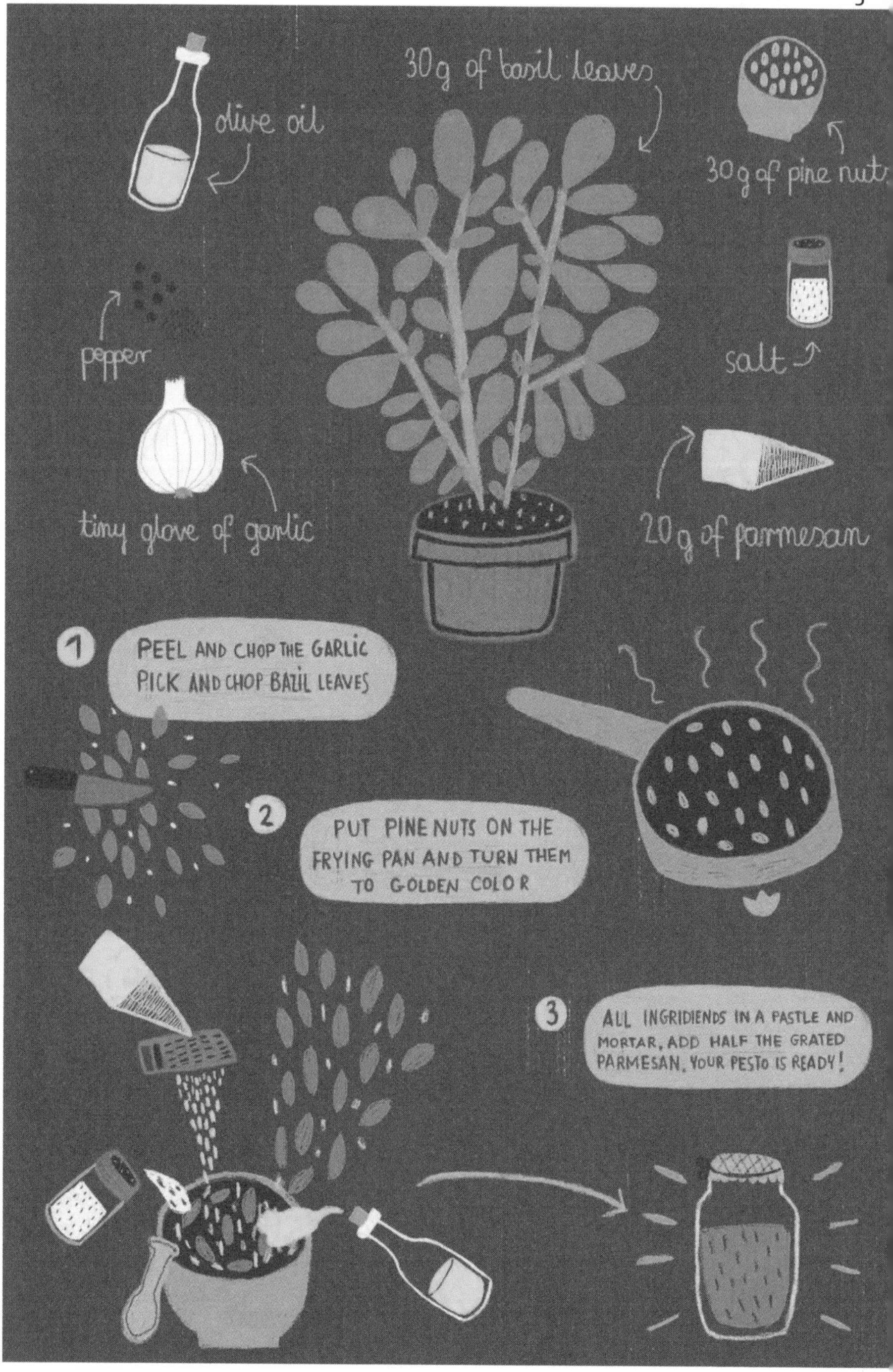
30g of basil leaves
olive oil
30g of pine nut
pepper
salt
tiny glove of garlic
20g of parmesan
1
PEEL AND CHOP THE GARLIC
PICK AND CHOP BAZIL LEAVES
2
PUT PINE NUTS ON THE FRYING PAN AND TURN THEM TO GOLDEN COLOR
3
ALL INGRIDIENDS IN A PASTLE AND MORTAR, ADD HALF THE GRATED PARMESAN. YOUR PESTO IS READY!

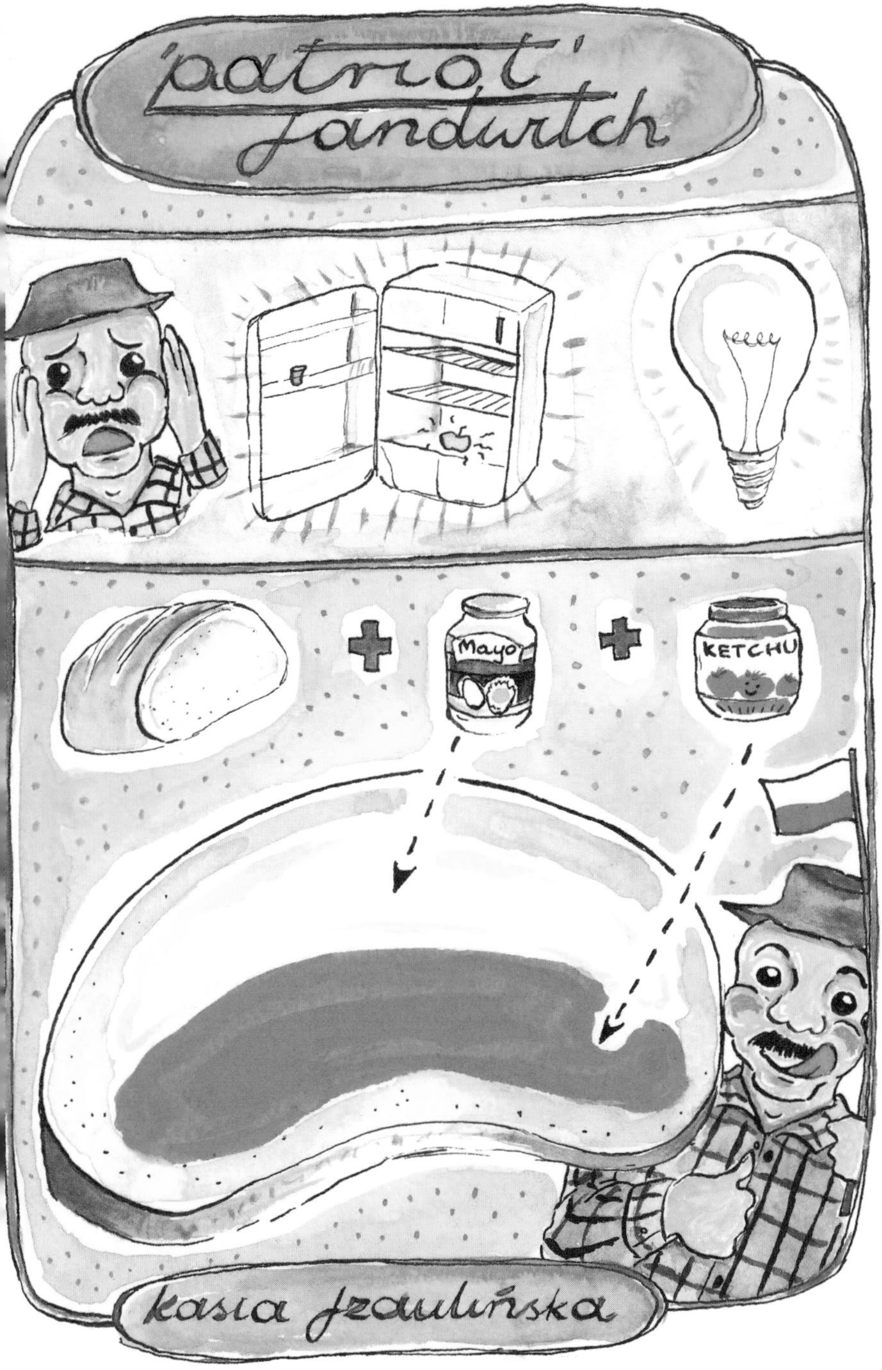
'patriot'
sandwitch
Mayo
KETCHU
kasia szaulińska

# salads

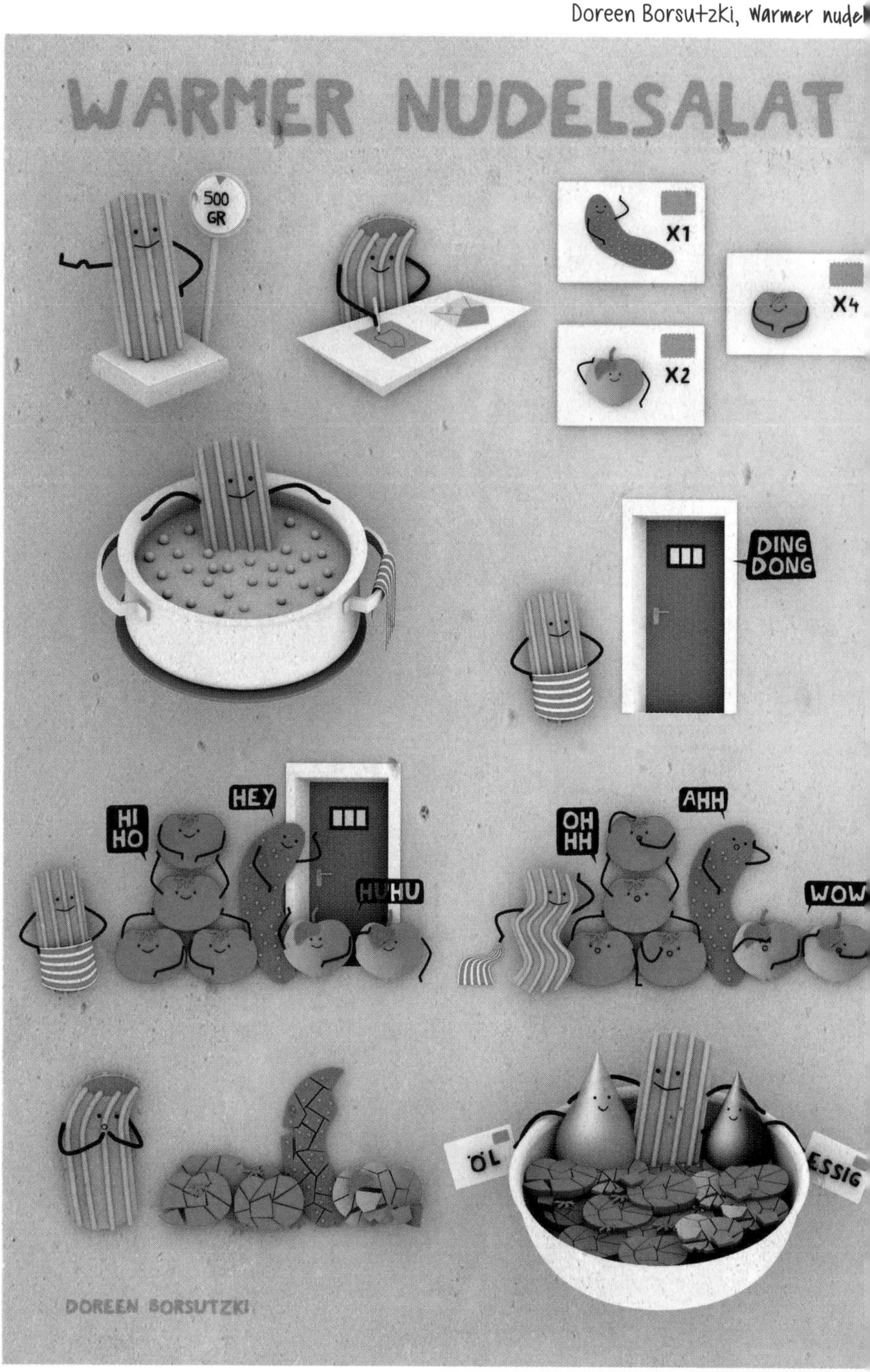
WARMER NUDELSALAT
500
GR
X1
X4
X2
DING
DONG
HI
HO
HEY
HUHU
OH
HH
AHH
WOW
ÖL
ESSIG
DOREEN BORSUTZKI

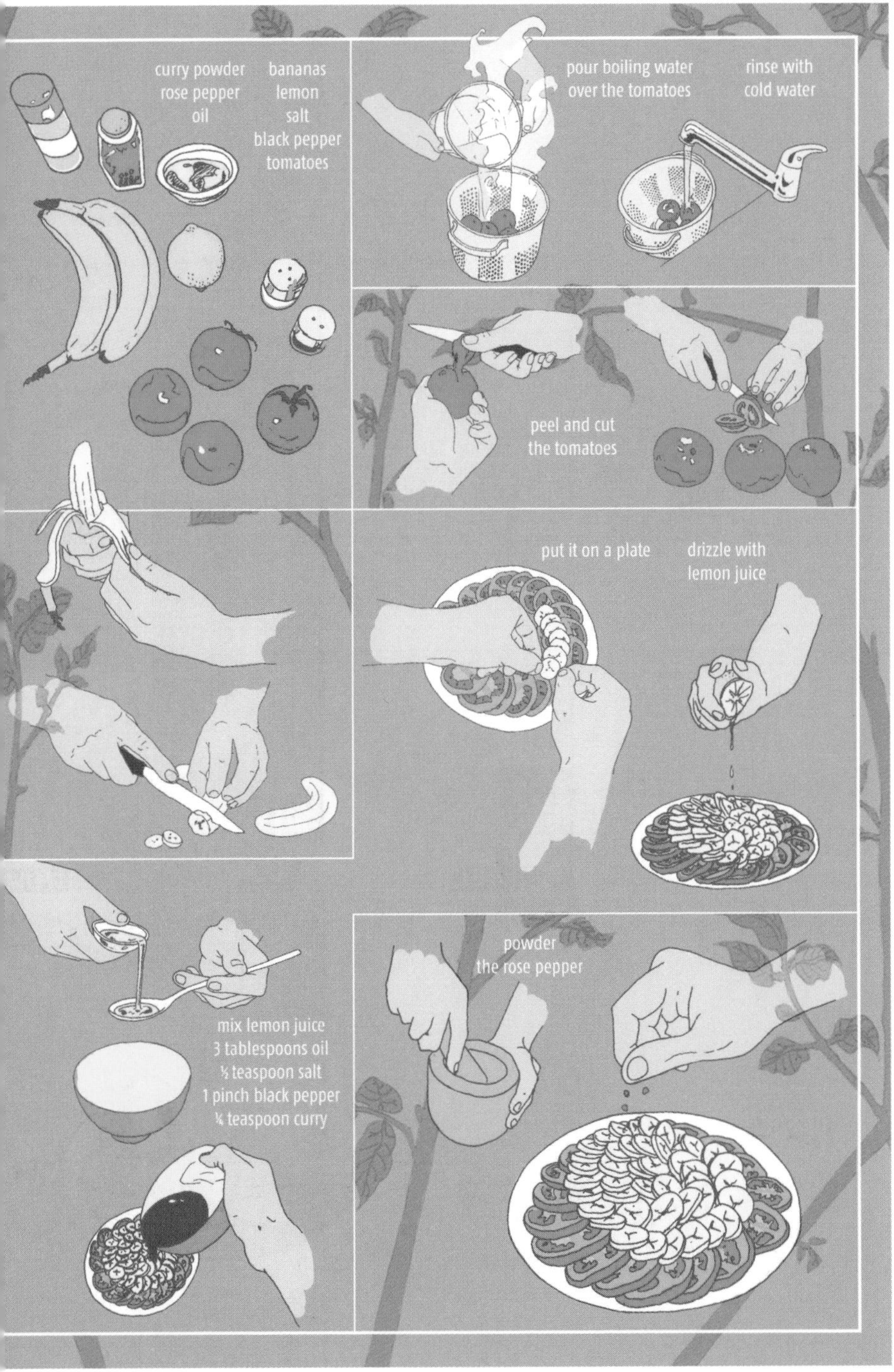
curry powder
rose pepper
oil
bananas
lemon
salt
black pepper
tomatoes
pour boiling water
over the tomatoes
rinse with
cold water
peel and cut
the tomatoes
put it on a plate
drizzle with
lemon juice
mix lemon juice
3 tablespoons oil
½ teaspoon salt
1 pinch black pepper
¼ teaspoon curry
powder
the rose pepper

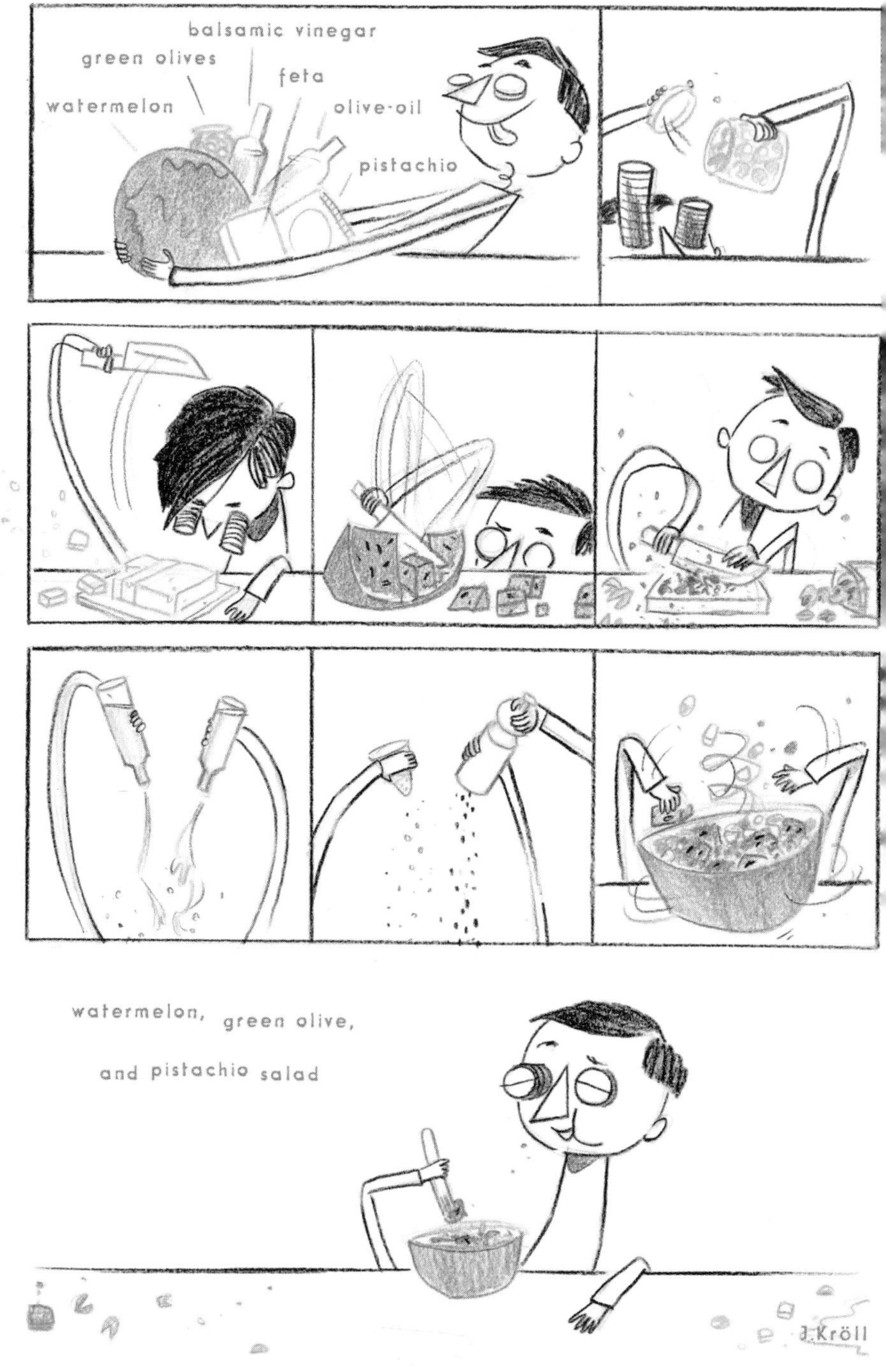
balsamic vinegar
green olives
watermelon
feta
olive-oil
pistachio
watermelon, green olive,
and pistachio salad
J.Kröll

## Salad with arugula and salmon

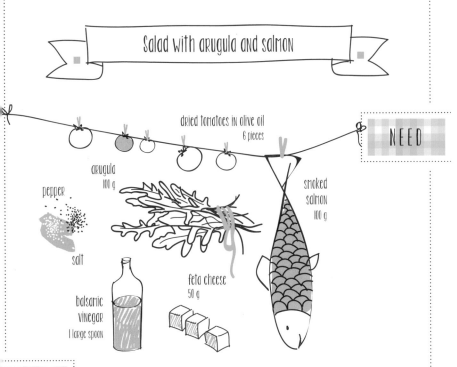

**NEED**

dried tomatoes in olive oil
6 pieces

arugula
100 g

pepper

salt

smoked
salmon
100 g

balsamic
vinegar
1 large spoon

feta cheese
50 g

**MAKE**

1. Wash and dry the arugula.

2. Cut smoked salmon and dried tomatoes (not too finely).

3. In a bowl, mix gently the arugula, tomatoes, feta cheese and salmon.

4. Spread the balsamic vinegar and season with salt and pepper. Mix it well.

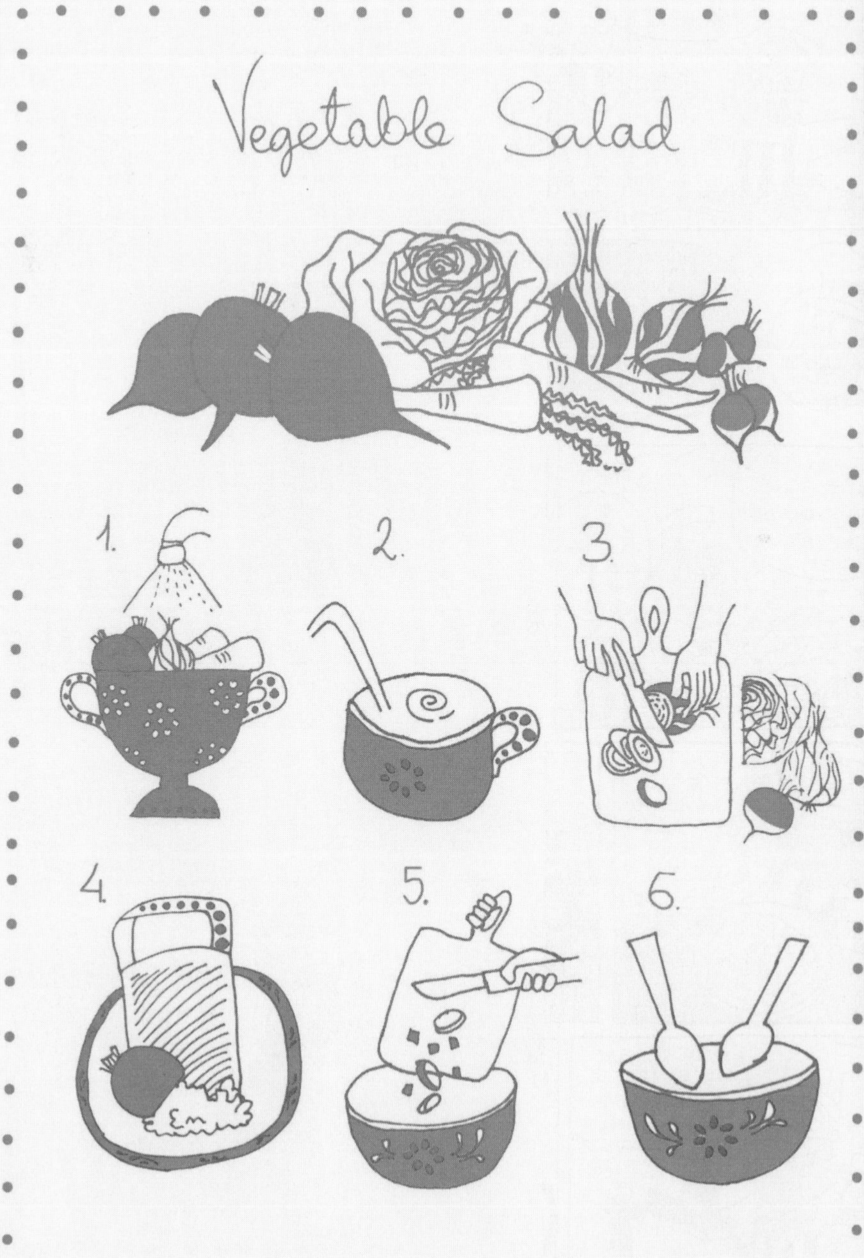
Vegetable Salad
1.
2.
3.
4.
5.
6.

soups

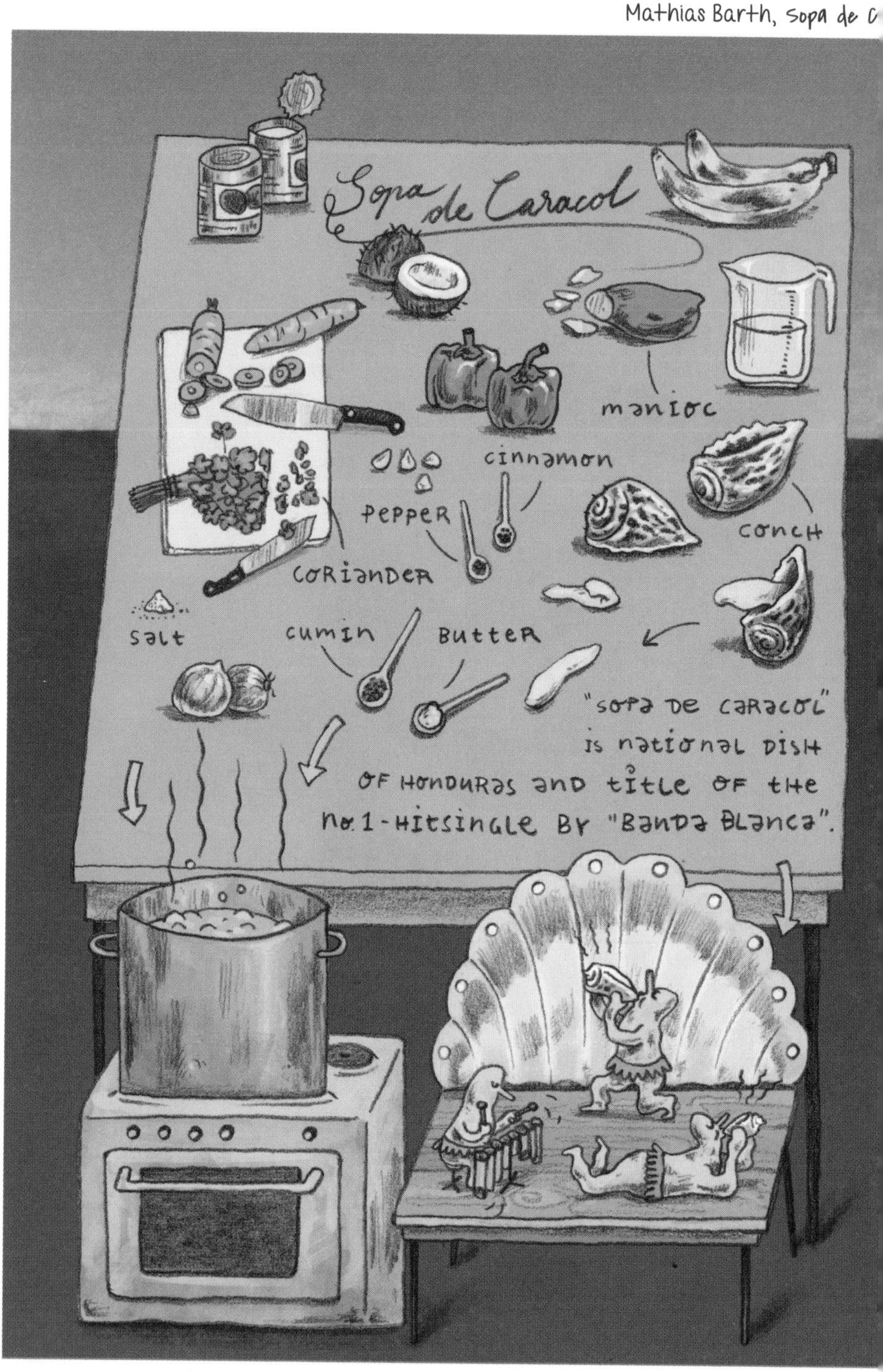
Sopa de Caracol
manioc
cinnamon
pepper
conch
coriander
salt
cumin
butter
"sopa de caracol" is national dish of Honduras and title of the no.1-hitsingle by "Banda Blanca".

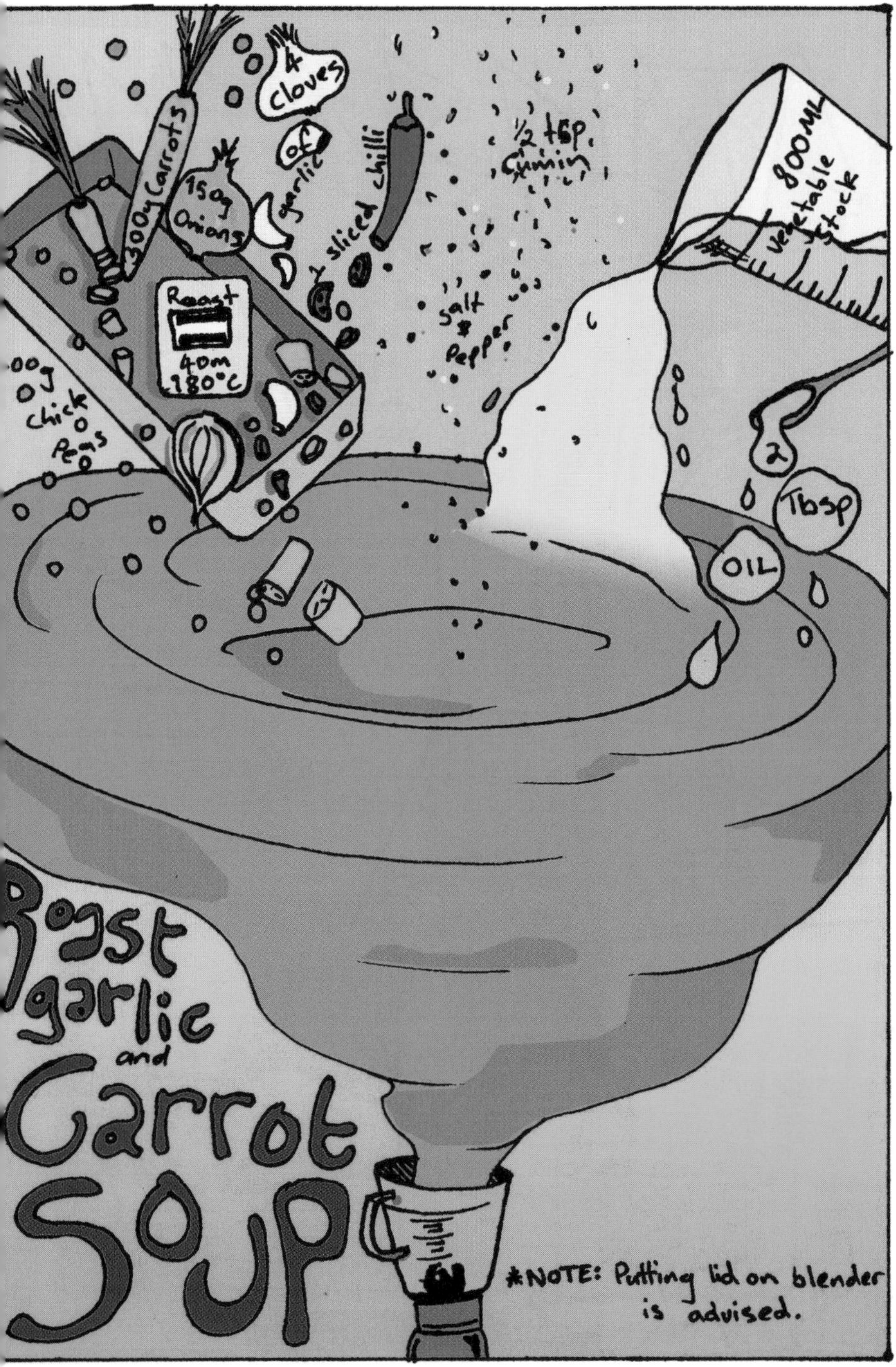

300g Carrots
150g Onions
4 cloves of garlic
1 sliced chilli
1/2 tbsp Cumin
salt & Pepper
800ML vegetable stock
2 Tbsp OIL
Roast 40m 180°C
00g chick Peas
Roast garlic and Carrot Soup
*NOTE: Putting lid on blender is advised.

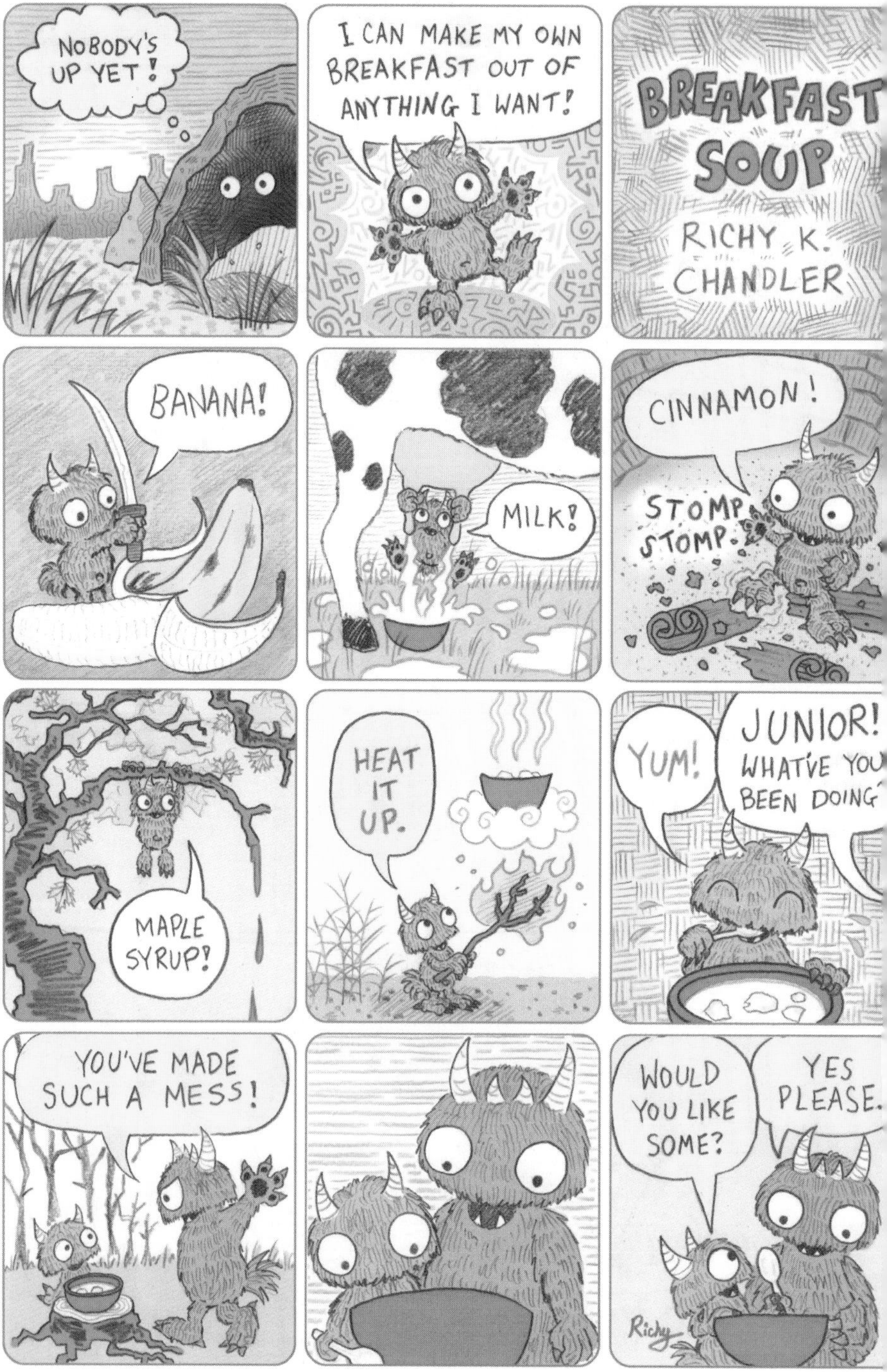
NOBODY'S UP YET!
I CAN MAKE MY OWN BREAKFAST OUT OF ANYTHING I WANT!
BREAKFAST SOUP
RICHY K. CHANDLER
BANANA!
MILK!
CINNAMON!
STOMP STOMP.
MAPLE SYRUP!
HEAT IT UP.
YUM!
JUNIOR! WHAT'VE YOU BEEN DOING
YOU'VE MADE SUCH A MESS!
WOULD YOU LIKE SOME?
YES PLEASE.
Richy

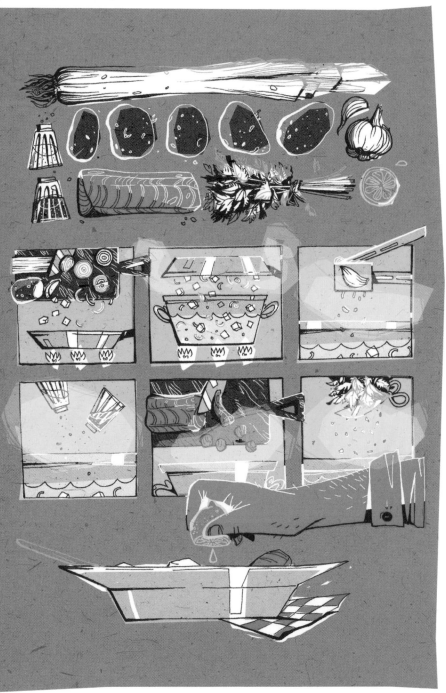

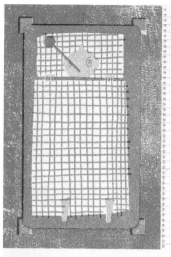

rosół
salt
leek
pepper
chicken
parsley
noodles
onion
thyme
rosemary
bay leaf
carrot
parsley root

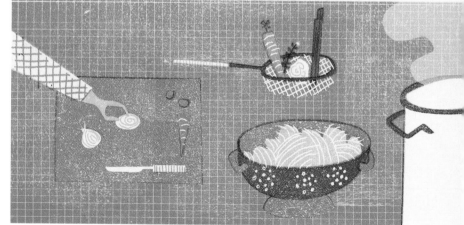

# INDIAN PUMPKINSOUP

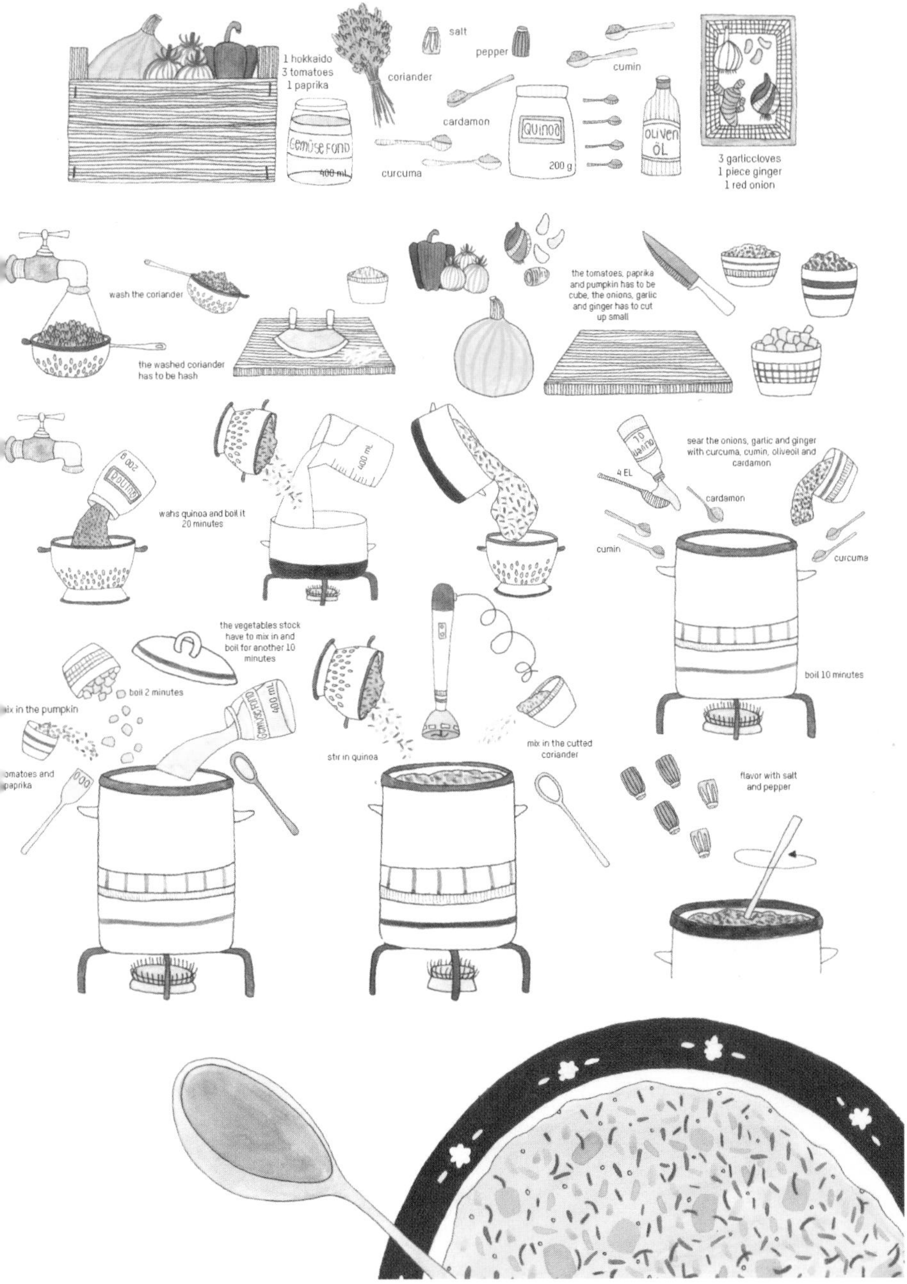

1 hokkaido
3 tomatoes
1 paprika
Gemüse Fond
400 mL
coriander
salt
pepper
cumin
cardamon
curcuma
Quinoa
200 g
Oliven Öl
3 garliccloves
1 piece ginger
1 red onion
wash the coriander
the washed coriander has to be hash
the tomatoes, paprika and pumpkin has to be cube, the onions, garlic and ginger has to cut up small
Quinoa
200 g
wahs quinoa and boil it 20 minutes
400 mL
sear the onions, garlic and ginger with curcuma, cumin, oliveoil and cardamon
4 EL
cardamon
cumin
curcuma
boil 10 minutes
the vegetables stock have to mix in and boil for another 10 minutes
boil 2 minutes
mix in the pumpkin
Gemüse Fond
400 mL
tomatoes and paprika
stir in quinoa
mix in the cutted coriander
flavor with salt and pepper

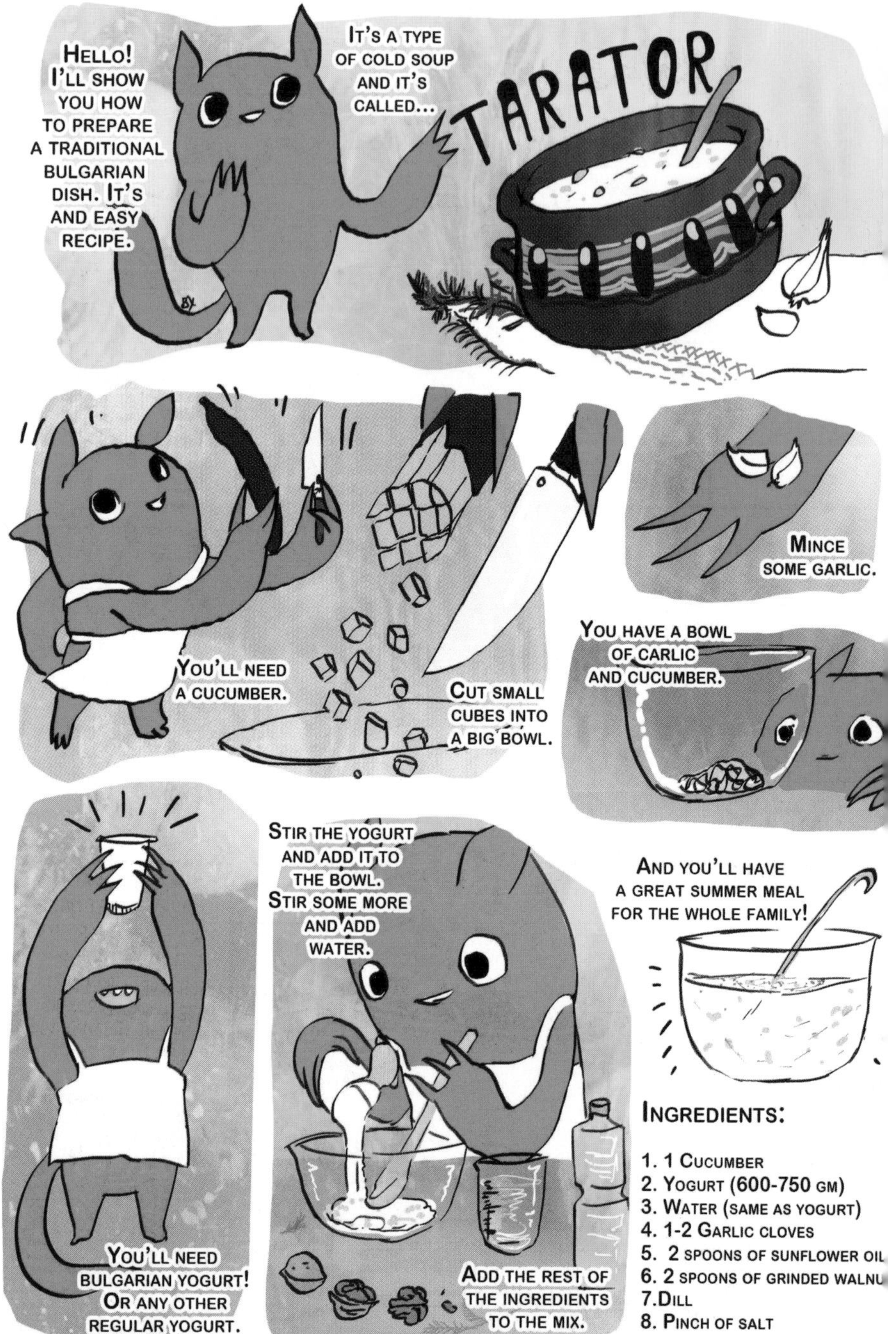
HELLO! I'LL SHOW YOU HOW TO PREPARE A TRADITIONAL BULGARIAN DISH. IT'S AND EASY RECIPE.
IT'S A TYPE OF COLD SOUP AND IT'S CALLED...
TARATOR
YOU'LL NEED A CUCUMBER.
CUT SMALL CUBES INTO A BIG BOWL.
MINCE SOME GARLIC.
YOU HAVE A BOWL OF CARLIC AND CUCUMBER.
YOU'LL NEED BULGARIAN YOGURT! OR ANY OTHER REGULAR YOGURT.
STIR THE YOGURT AND ADD IT TO THE BOWL. STIR SOME MORE AND ADD WATER.
ADD THE REST OF THE INGREDIENTS TO THE MIX.
AND YOU'LL HAVE A GREAT SUMMER MEAL FOR THE WHOLE FAMILY!
INGREDIENTS:
1. 1 CUCUMBER
2. YOGURT (600-750 GM)
3. WATER (SAME AS YOGURT)
4. 1-2 GARLIC CLOVES
5. 2 SPOONS OF SUNFLOWER OIL
6. 2 SPOONS OF GRINDED WALNU
7.DILL
8. PINCH OF SALT

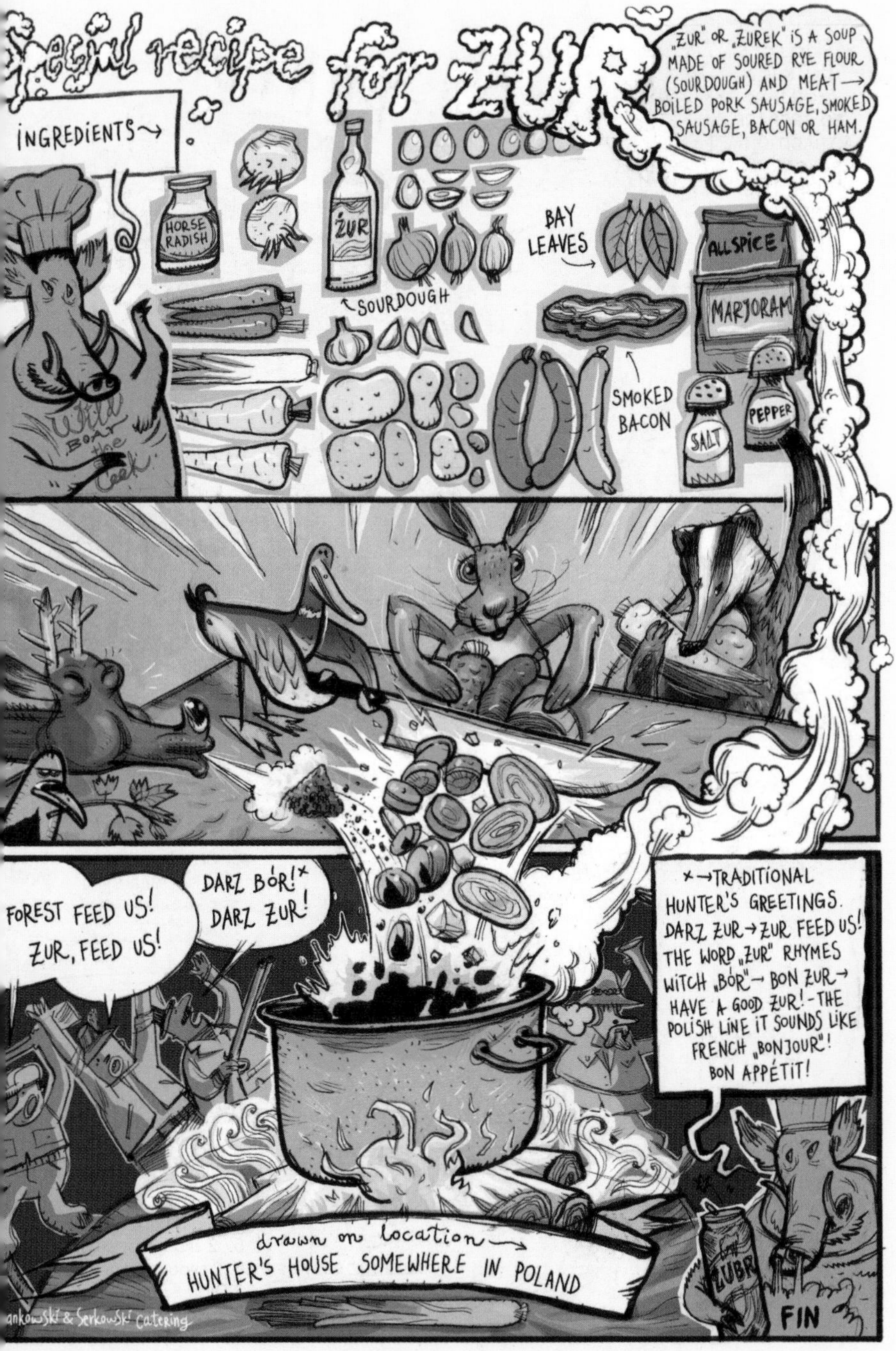
Special recipe for ŻUR
"ŻUR" OR "ŻUREK" IS A SOUP MADE OF SOURED RYE FLOUR (SOURDOUGH) AND MEAT → BOILED PORK SAUSAGE, SMOKED SAUSAGE, BACON OR HAM.
INGREDIENTS →
HORSE RADISH
ŻUR
SOURDOUGH
BAY LEAVES
ALLSPICE
MARJORAM
SMOKED BACON
SALT
PEPPER
Wild Boar the Cook
FOREST FEED US! ŻUR, FEED US!
DARZ BÓR!* DARZ ŻUR!
* → TRADITIONAL HUNTER'S GREETINGS. DARZ ŻUR → ŻUR FEED US! THE WORD "ŻUR" RHYMES WITCH "BÓR" → BON ŻUR → HAVE A GOOD ŻUR! - THE POLISH LINE IT SOUNDS LIKE FRENCH "BONJOUR"! BON APPÉTIT!
drawn on location →
HUNTER'S HOUSE SOMEWHERE IN POLAND
ŻUBR
FIN
Jankowski & Serkowski catering

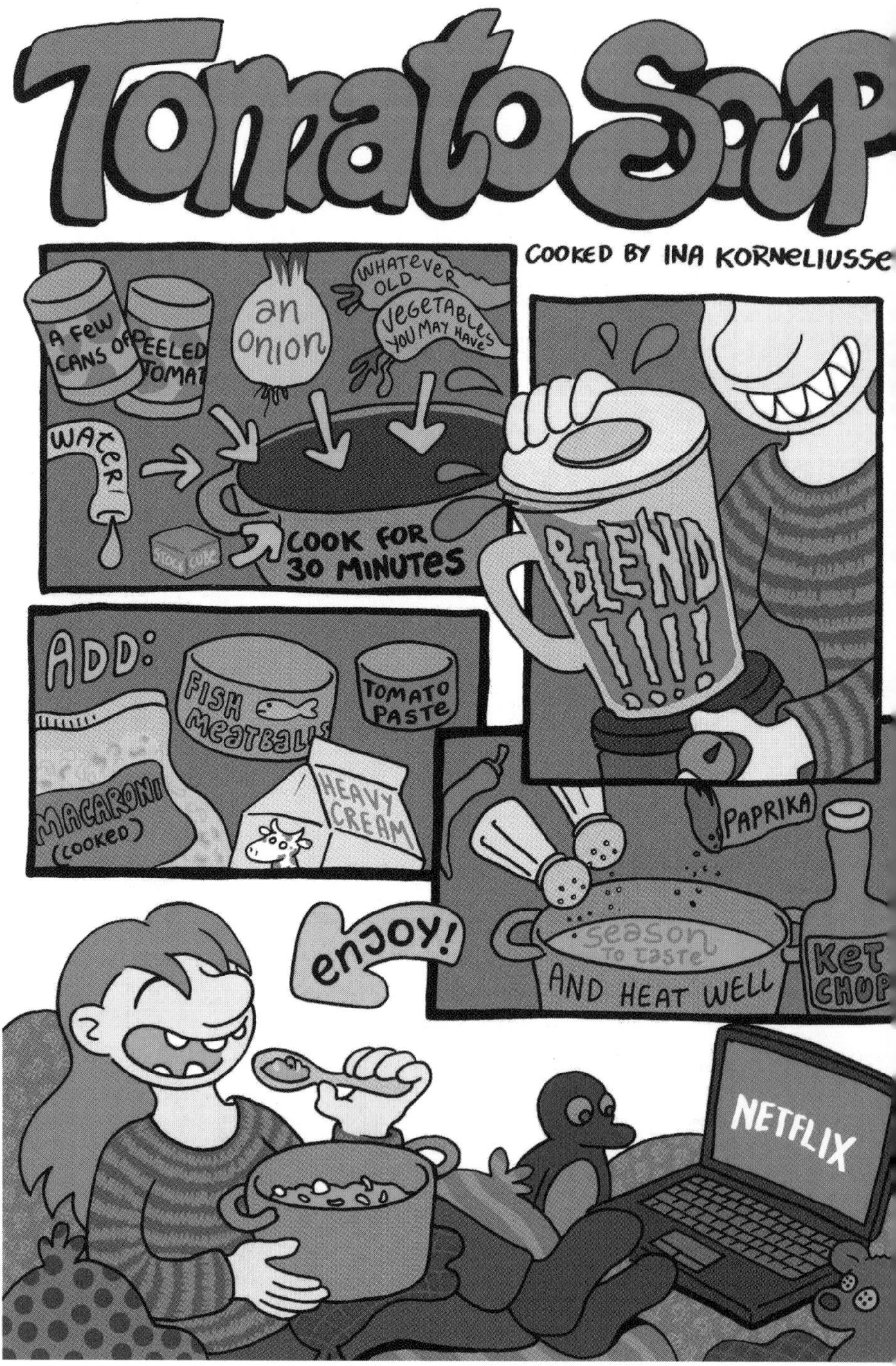
Tomato Soup
COOKED BY INA KORNELIUSSE
A FEW CANS OF
PEELED TOMAT
an onion
WHATEVER OLD
VEGETABLES YOU MAY HAVE
WATER
STOCK CUBE
COOK FOR 30 MINUTES
BLEND!!!!
ADD:
FISH MEATBALLS
TOMATO PASTE
MACARONI (COOKED)
HEAVY CREAM
PAPRIKA
season to taste
AND HEAT WELL
KET CHUP
enJOY!
NETFLIX

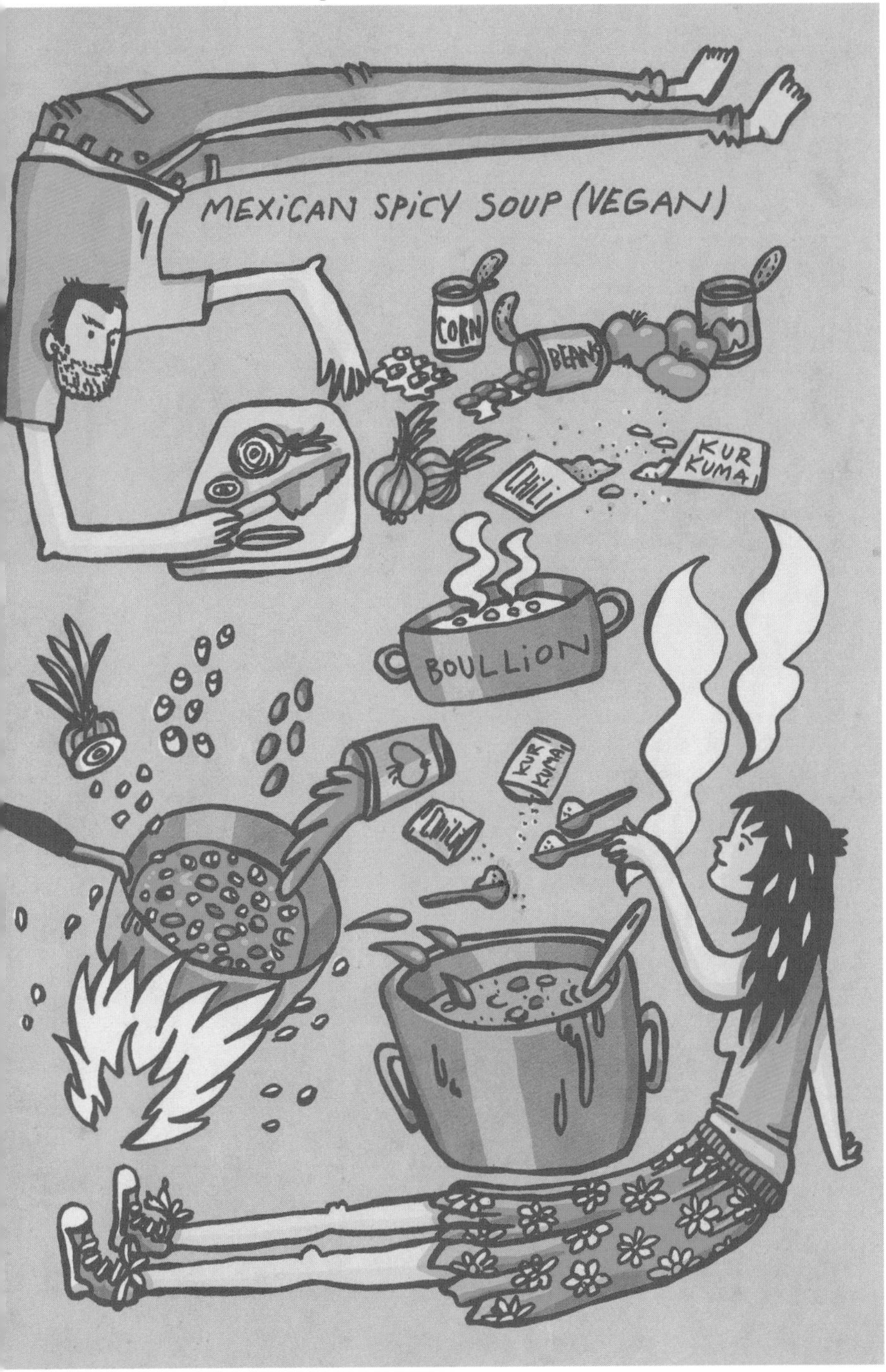
MEXICAN SPICY SOUP (VEGAN)
CORN
BEANS
KUR KUMA
CHILI
BOULLION
KUR KUMA
CHILI

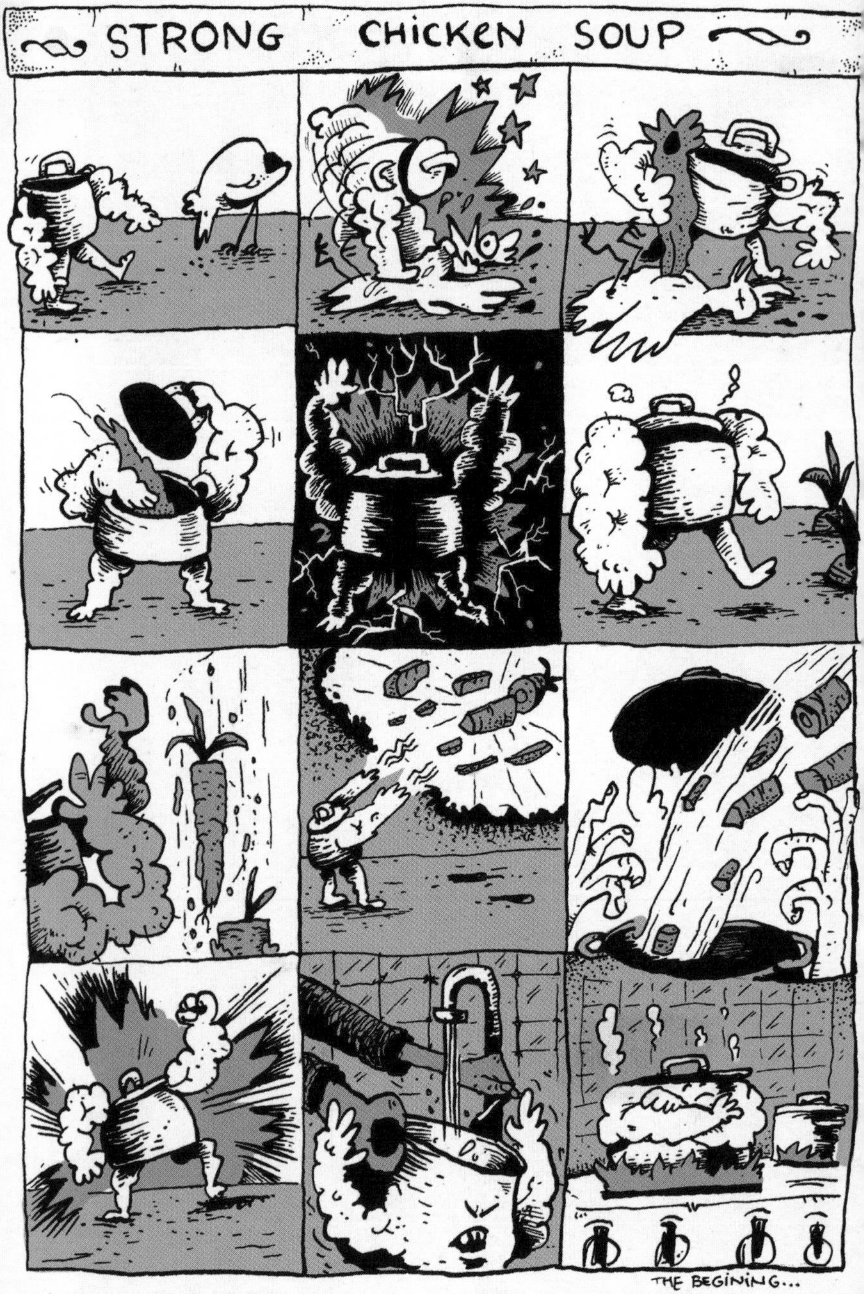
STRONG CHICKEN SOUP
THE BEGINING...

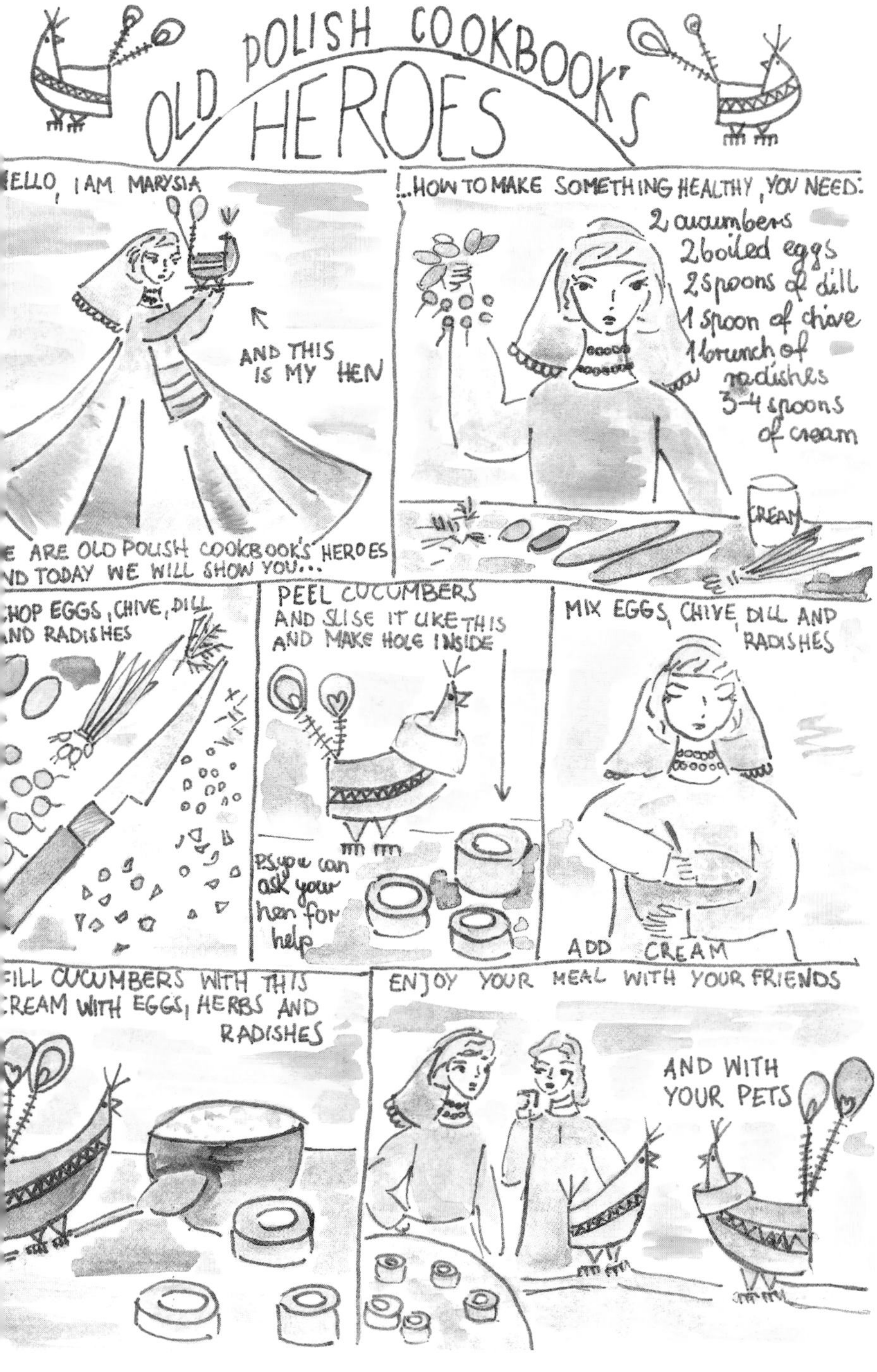
OLD POLISH COOKBOOK'S HEROES
ELLO, I AM MARYSIA
AND THIS IS MY HEN
E ARE OLD POLISH COOKBOOK'S HEROES
D TODAY WE WILL SHOW YOU...
...HOW TO MAKE SOMETHING HEALTHY, YOU NEED:
2 cucumbers
2 boiled eggs
2 spoons of dill
1 spoon of chive
1 brunch of radishes
3-4 spoons of cream
CREAM
HOP EGGS, CHIVE, DILL
ND RADISHES
PEEL CUCUMBERS
AND SLISE IT LIKE THIS
AND MAKE HOLE INSIDE
P.S. you can ask your hen for help
MIX EGGS, CHIVE, DILL AND RADISHES
ADD CREAM
ILL CUCUMBERS WITH THIS
REAM WITH EGGS, HERBS AND RADISHES
ENJOY YOUR MEAL WITH YOUR FRIENDS
AND WITH YOUR PETS

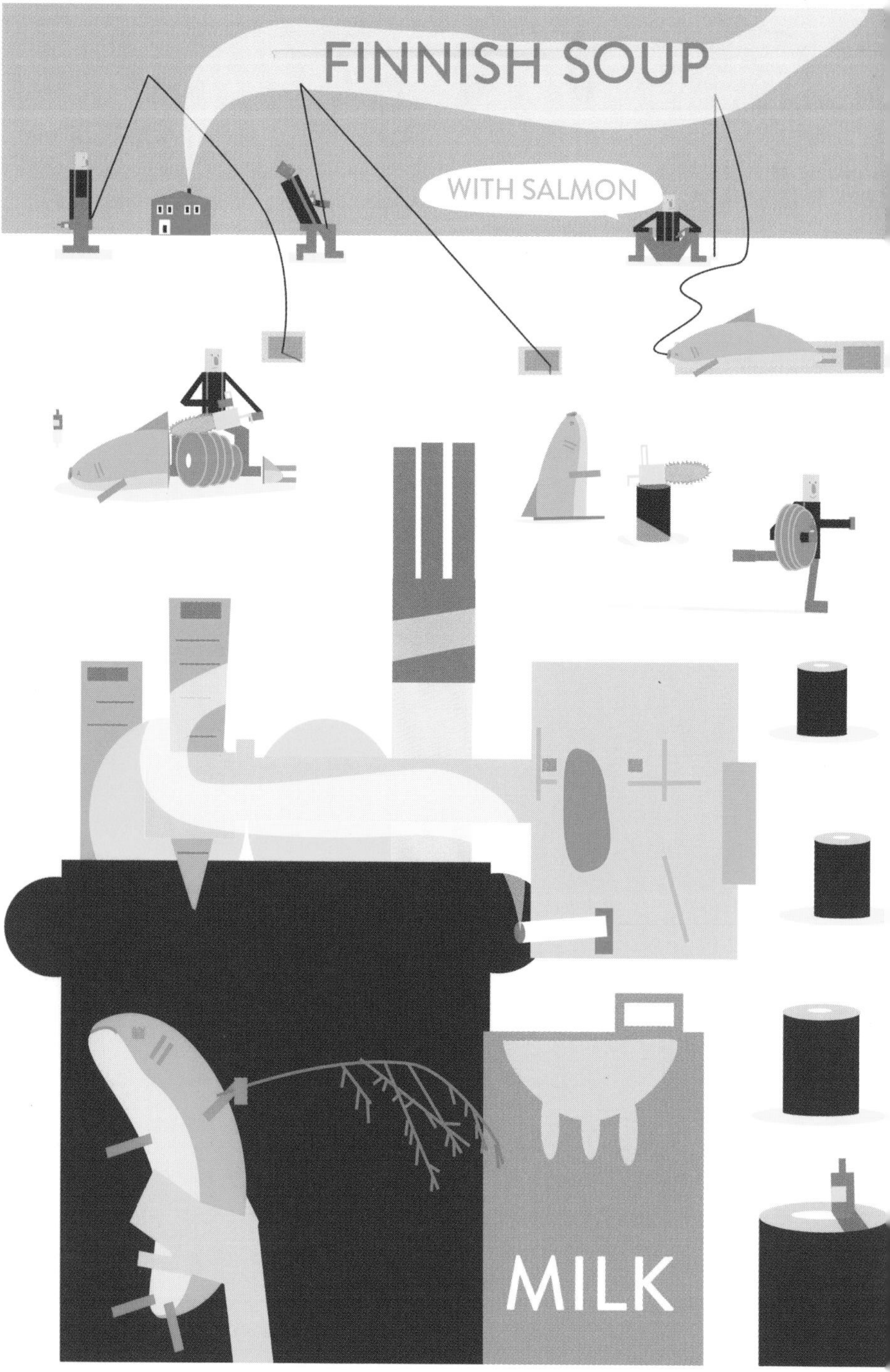
FINNISH SOUP
WITH SALMON
MILK

arzyna Urbaniak, Chicken Broth

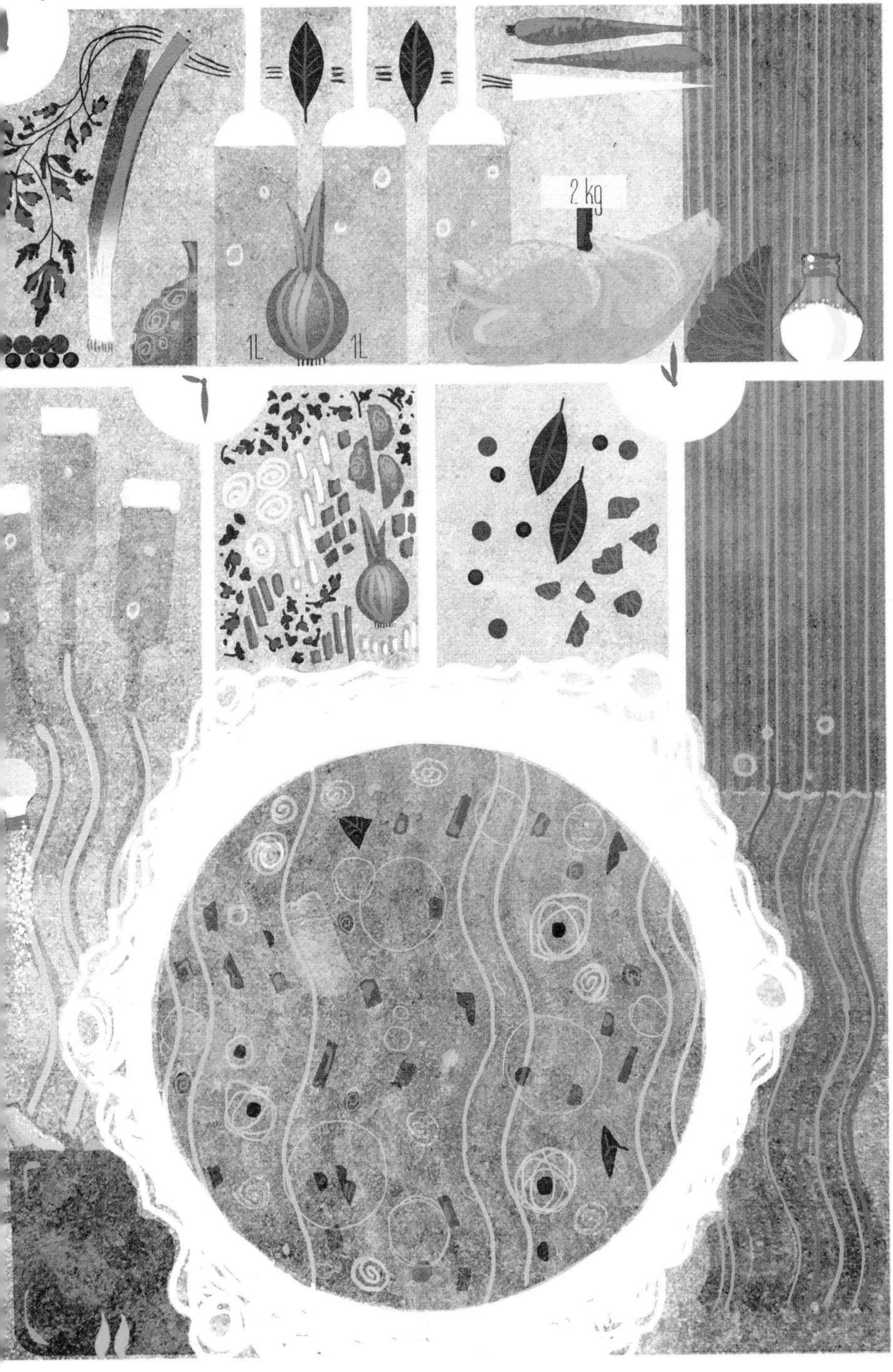

2 kg
1L
1L

main courses

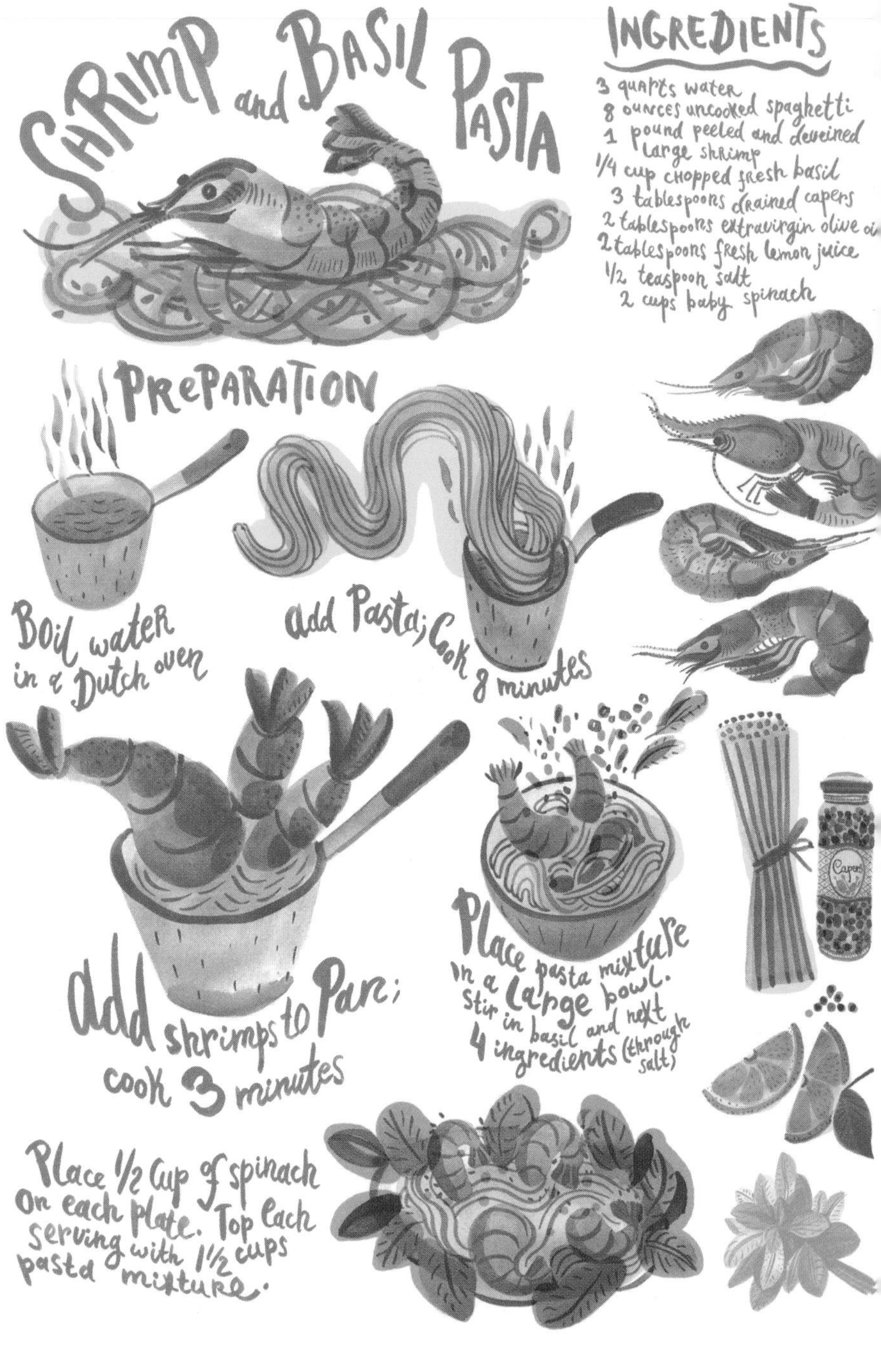
SHRIMP and BASIL PASTA
INGREDIENTS
3 quarts water
8 ounces uncooked spaghetti
1 pound peeled and deveined large shrimp
1/4 cup chopped fresh basil
3 tablespoons drained capers
2 tablespoons extravirgin olive oi
2 tablespoons fresh lemon juice
1/2 teaspoon salt
2 cups baby spinach
PREPARATION
Boil water in a Dutch oven
add Pasta; Cook 8 minutes
add shrimps to Pan; cook 3 minutes
Place pasta mixture in a large bowl. Stir in basil and next 4 ingredients (through salt)
Capers
Place 1/2 Cup of spinach On each plate. Top each serving with 1 1/2 cups pasta mixture.

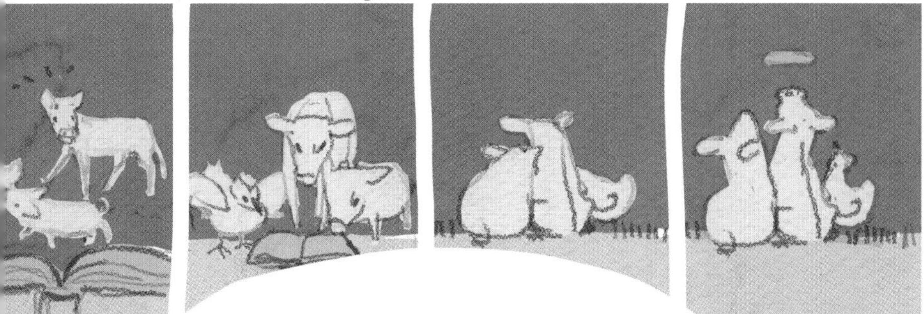

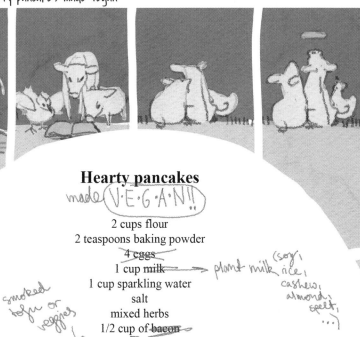

# Hearty pancakes

made V·E·G·A·N!!

2 cups flour
2 teaspoons baking powder
~~4 eggs~~
1 cup ~~milk~~ → plant milk (soy, rice, cashew, almond, spelt, ...)
1 cup sparkling water
salt
mixed herbs
1/2 cup of ~~bacon~~ ← smoked tofu or veggies

Mix all wet ingredients and add to dry ingredients.
Fry in ~~butter~~ marge or canola oil from both sides.

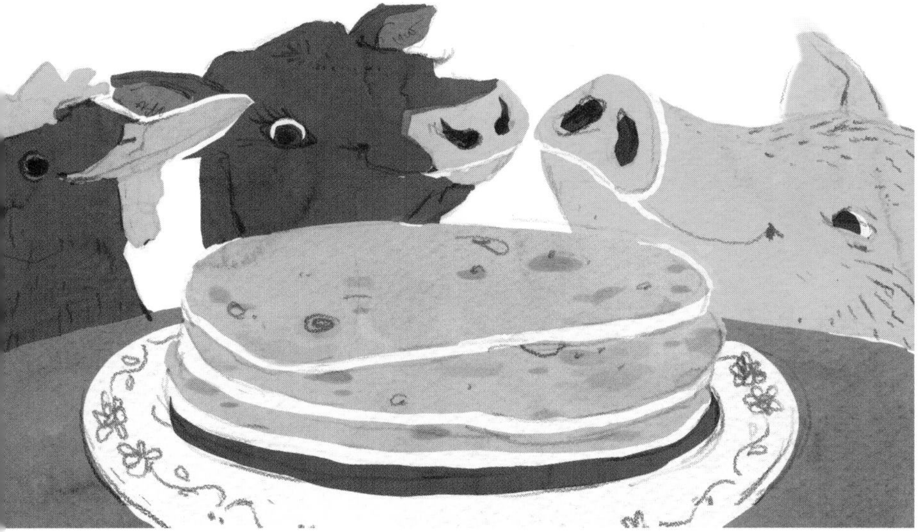

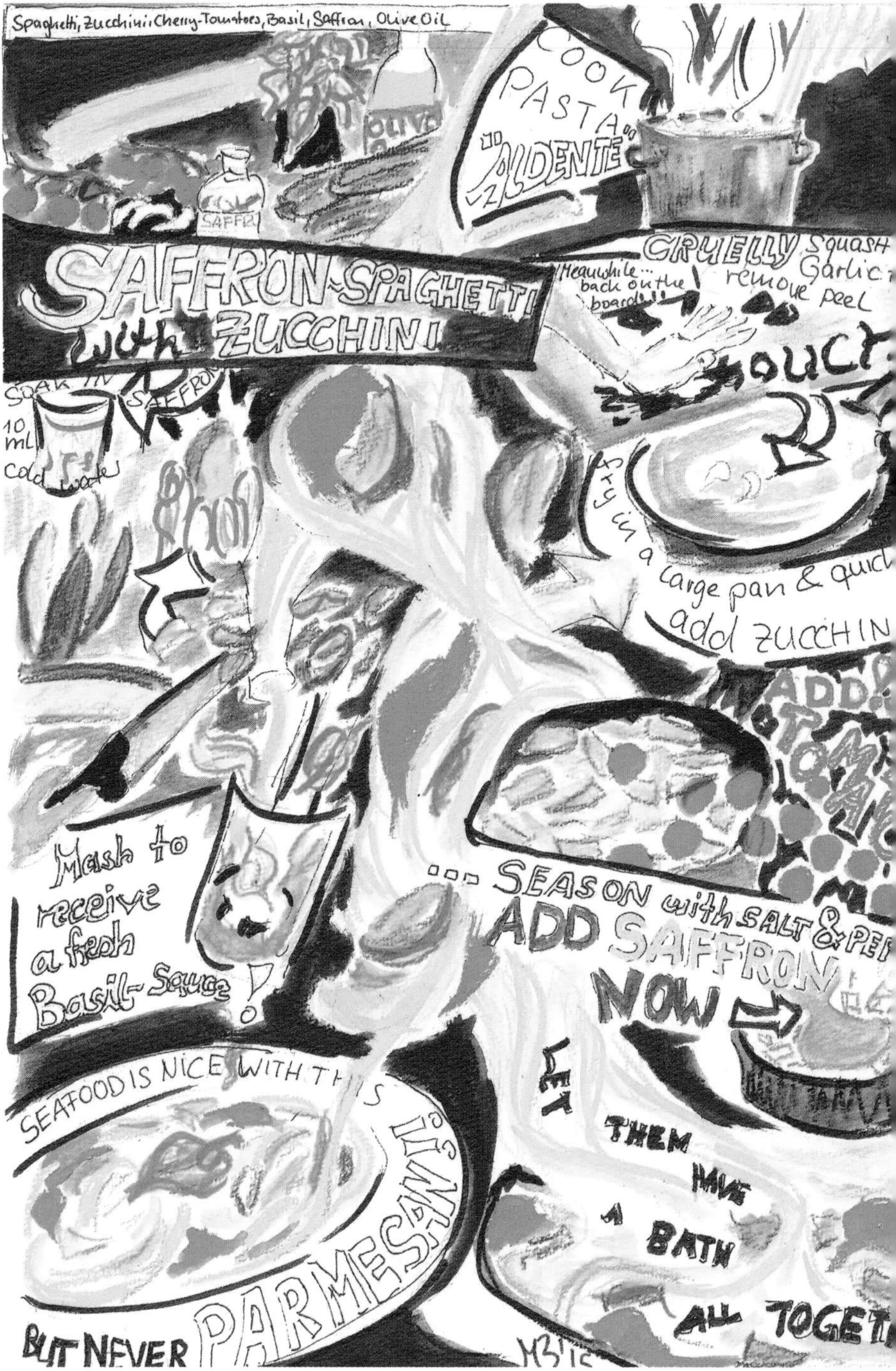
Spaghetti, Zucchini, Cherry-Tomatoes, Basil, Saffron, Olive Oil
SAFFRON-SPAGHETTI with ZUCCHINI
COOK PASTA "ALDENTE"
CRUELLY squash Garlic remove peel
Meanwhile... back on the board!!!
OUCH
SOAK IN SAFFRON
10 mL cold water
fry in a large pan & quick add ZUCCHINI
ADD TOMATOES
Mash to receive a fresh Basil-Sauce!
... SEASON with SALT & PEP
ADD SAFFRON NOW
LET THEM HAVE A BATH ALL TOGET
SEAFOOD IS NICE WITH THIS
BUT NEVER PARMESAN!!!

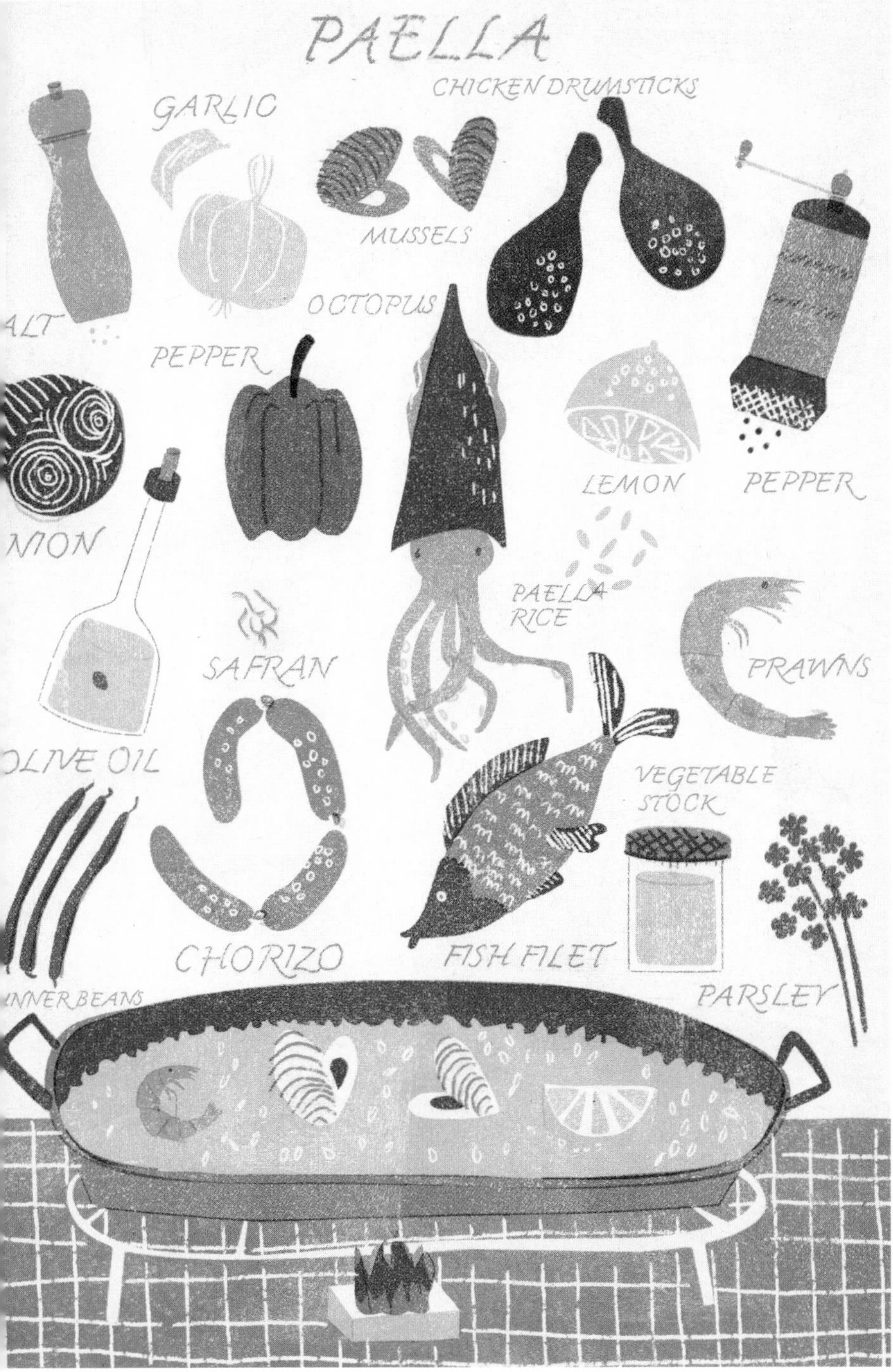
PAELLA
CHICKEN DRUMSTICKS
GARLIC
MUSSELS
ALT
OCTOPUS
PEPPER
LEMON
PEPPER
NION
PAELLA
RICE
SAFRAN
PRAWNS
OLIVE OIL
VEGETABLE
STOCK
CHORIZO
FISH FILET
INNER BEANS
PARSLEY

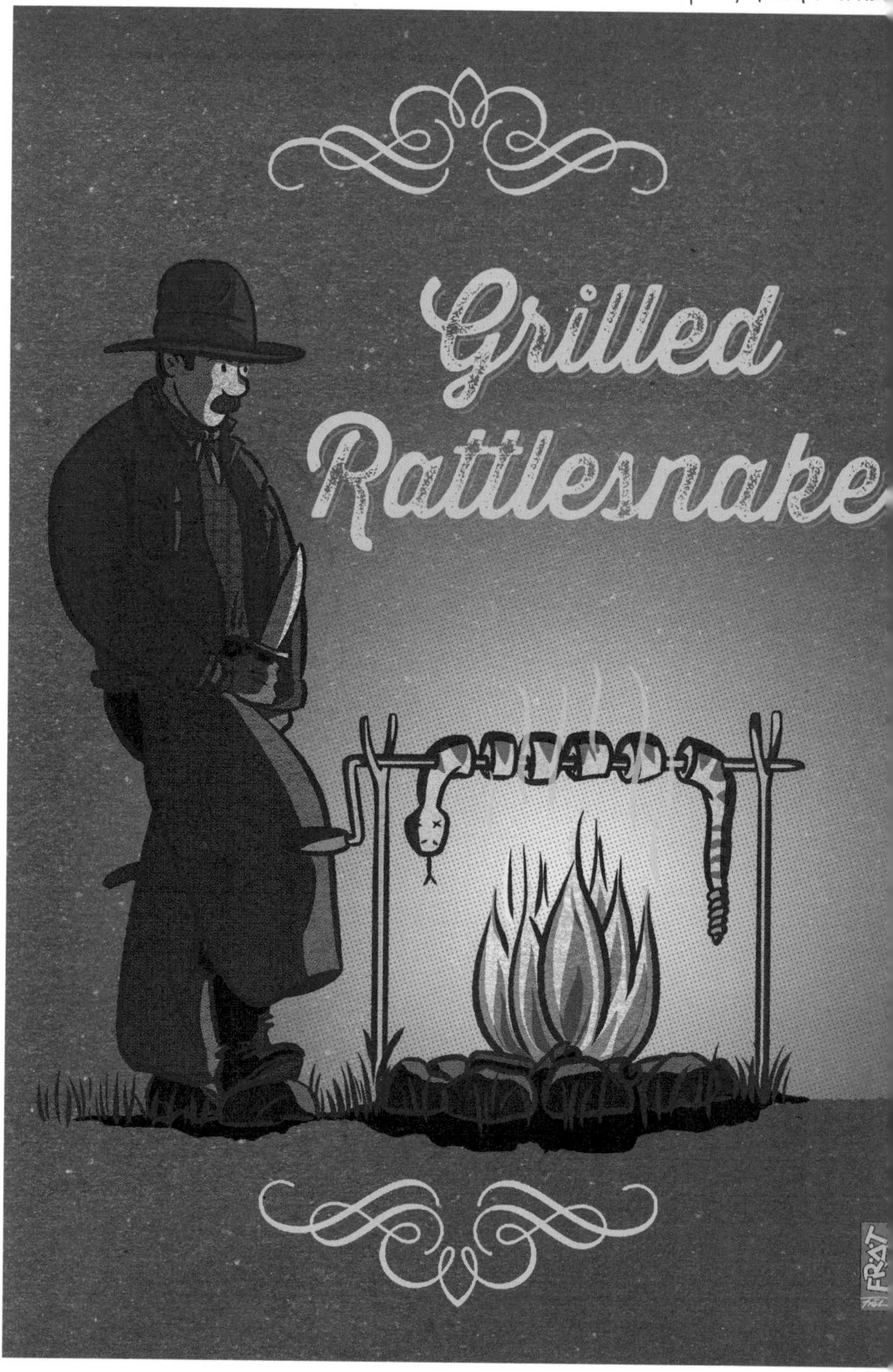
Grilled
Rattlesnake
FRAT

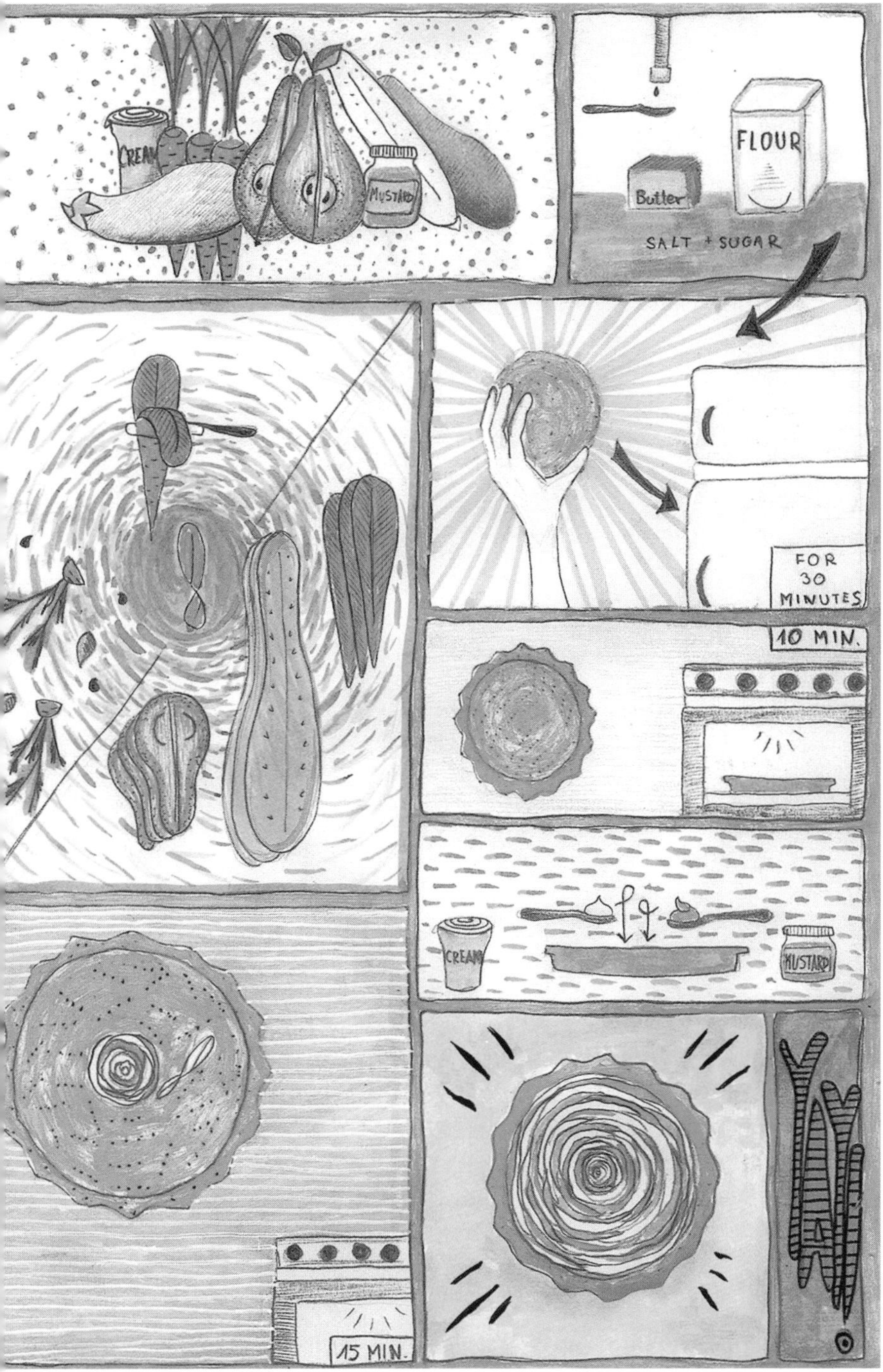
CREAM
MUSTARD
Butter
FLOUR
SALT + SUGAR
FOR 30 MINUTES
10 MIN.
CREAM
MUSTARD
15 MIN.

# DJ Cat Gosshie in KKK by HARUKICHI

# KKKの猫DJゴッシー

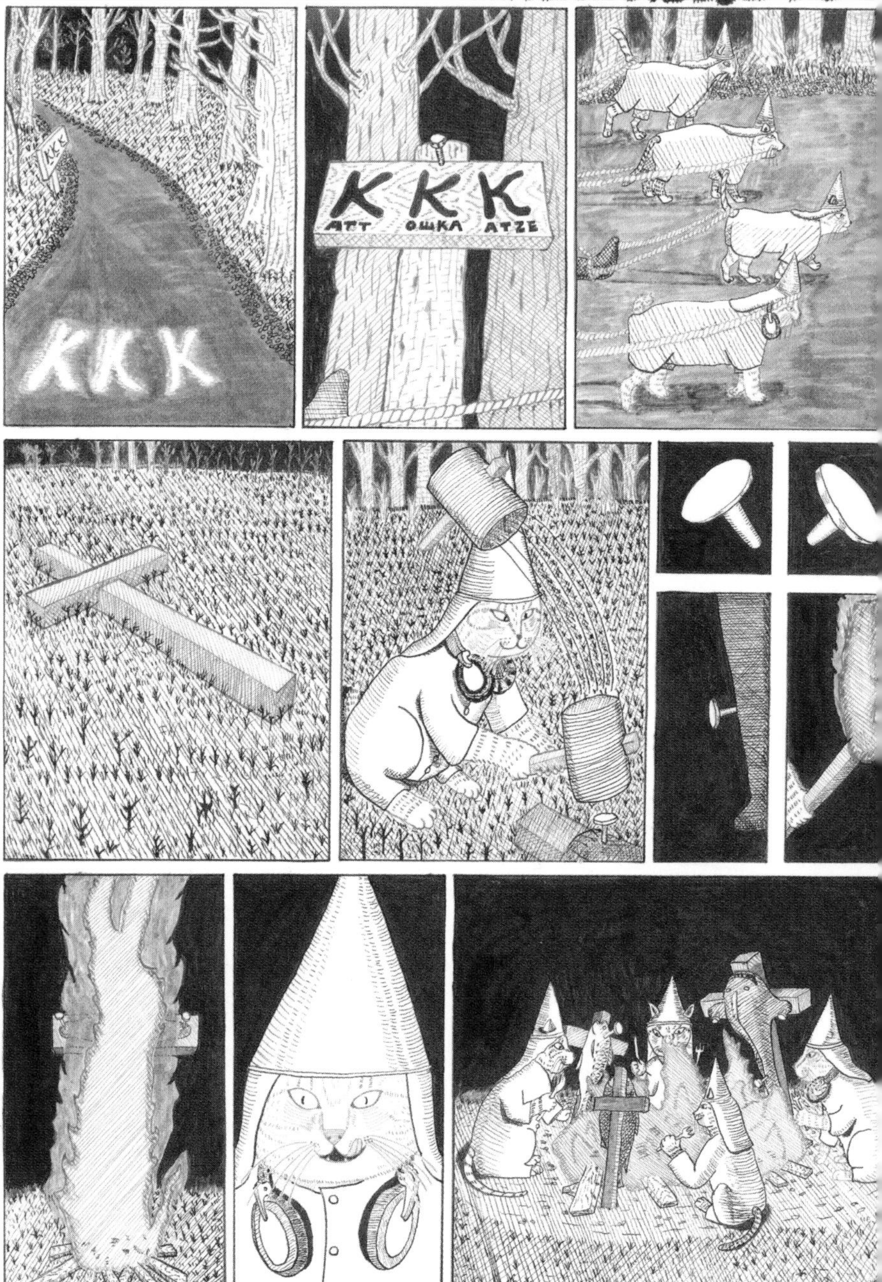
KKK
KKK
KKK
ATT OШKA ATZE

end 終

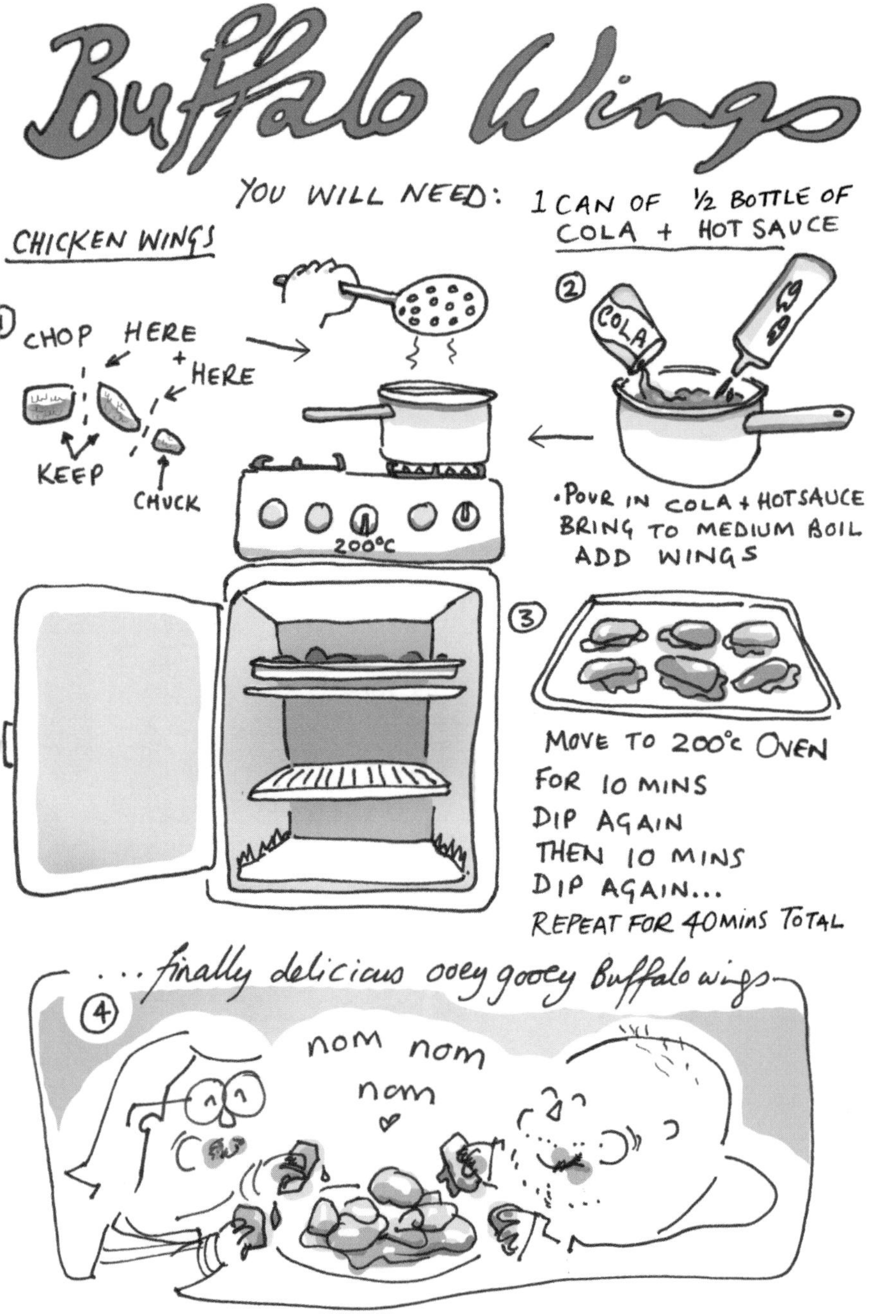
Buffalo Wings
YOU WILL NEED:
CHICKEN WINGS
1 CAN OF COLA +
½ BOTTLE OF HOT SAUCE
1
CHOP HERE + HERE
KEEP
CHUCK
2
COLA
200°C
• POUR IN COLA + HOTSAUCE
BRING TO MEDIUM BOIL
ADD WINGS
3
MOVE TO 200°C OVEN
FOR 10 MINS
DIP AGAIN
THEN 10 MINS
DIP AGAIN...
REPEAT FOR 40 MINS TOTAL
... finally delicious ooey gooey Buffalo wings
4
nom nom
nom

# HAI XIAN ZHOU

## CHINESE SEAFOOD RICE SOUP

SERVES FOUR - THANKS TO OUR FRIEND PEIRAN FOR THE RECIPE!

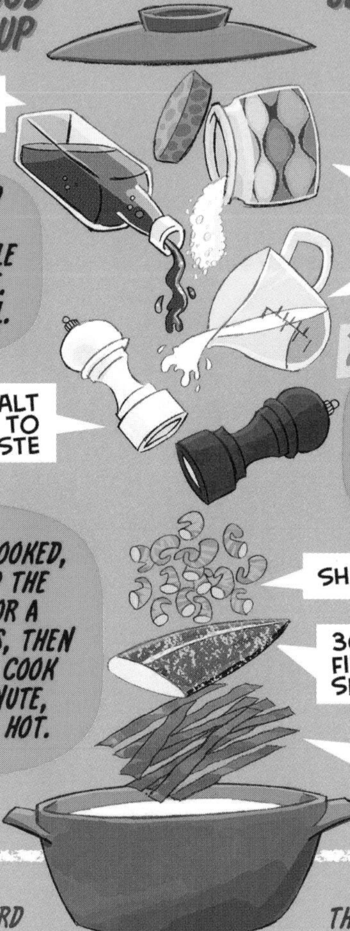

EXTRA VIRGIN OLIVE OIL: 20ML

SUSHI OR PUDDING RICE: 100G

WATER: 2 LITRES

A PINCH OF SALT AND PEPPER TO TASTE

SHRIMPS: 300G

300G COD FILLET, FINELY AND THINLY SLICED

HALF AN ICEBERG LETTUCE, FINELY SLICED

1: POUR THE OIL AND WATER INTO A STOVETOP CASSEROLE AND ADD THE RICE. BRING TO THE BOIL.

2: COVER THE CASSEROLE AND TURN DOWN THE HEAT. LEAVE THE RICE TO COOK UNTIL SOFT. STIR OCCASIONALLY.

3: WHEN THE RICE IS COOKED, ADD THE SALT AND THE SEAFOOD. COOK FOR A FURTHER 3-5 MINUTES, THEN ADD THE CABBAGE. COOK FOR ONE MORE MINUTE, THEN SERVE WHILE HOT.

*THERE'S NO STANDARD RECIPE TO FOLLOW - SCALLOPS, SEA BASS FILLETS, SALMON OR SQUID (ALL FINELY SLICED) WORK WELL IN THIS RECIPE. TRY MIXING & MATCHING!*

*FOR A MORE AUTHENTIC CHINESE TASTE, TRY ADDING FINELY SLICED GINGER, OR FINELY CHOPPED CHIVES OR SPRING ONIONS - OR EVEN BOTH TOGETHER!*

*THE TOTAL COOKING TIME IS AROUND 1 HOUR. IF YOU'RE WORRIED ABOUT BURNING THE RICE, TRY PLACING A METAL OR CERAMIC SPOON AT THE BOTTOM OF THE CASSEROLE - THIS ACTUALLY WORKS!*

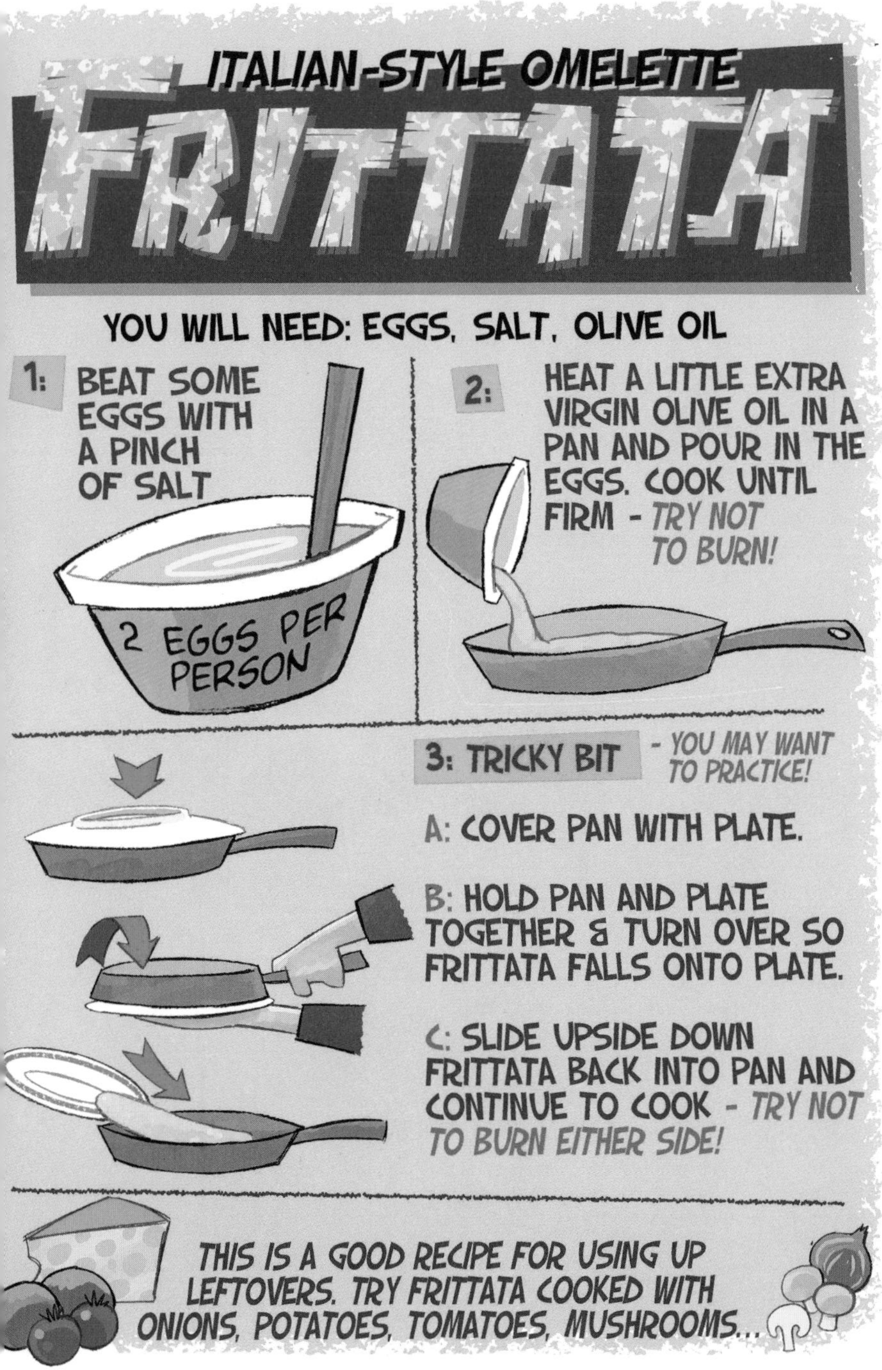
ITALIAN-STYLE OMELETTE
FRITTATA
YOU WILL NEED: EGGS, SALT, OLIVE OIL
1: BEAT SOME EGGS WITH A PINCH OF SALT
2 EGGS PER PERSON
2: HEAT A LITTLE EXTRA VIRGIN OLIVE OIL IN A PAN AND POUR IN THE EGGS. COOK UNTIL FIRM - TRY NOT TO BURN!
3: TRICKY BIT - YOU MAY WANT TO PRACTICE!
A: COVER PAN WITH PLATE.
B: HOLD PAN AND PLATE TOGETHER & TURN OVER SO FRITTATA FALLS ONTO PLATE.
C: SLIDE UPSIDE DOWN FRITTATA BACK INTO PAN AND CONTINUE TO COOK - TRY NOT TO BURN EITHER SIDE!
THIS IS A GOOD RECIPE FOR USING UP LEFTOVERS. TRY FRITTATA COOKED WITH ONIONS, POTATOES, TOMATOES, MUSHROOMS...

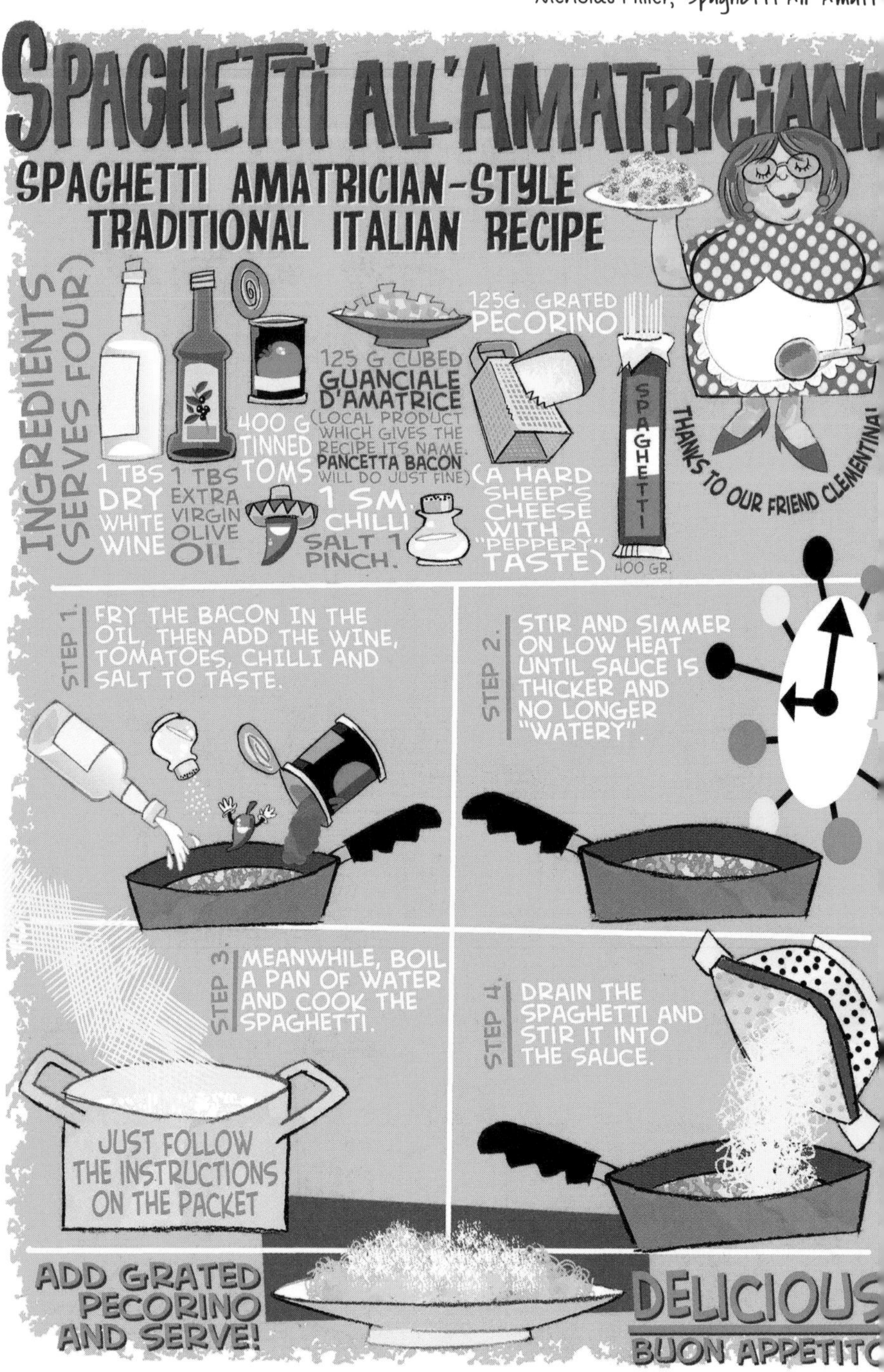
SPAGHETTI ALL'AMATRICIANA
SPAGHETTI AMATRICIAN-STYLE
TRADITIONAL ITALIAN RECIPE
INGREDIENTS (SERVES FOUR)
1 TBS DRY WHITE WINE
1 TBS EXTRA VIRGIN OLIVE OIL
400 G TINNED TOMS
125 G CUBED GUANCIALE D'AMATRICE (LOCAL PRODUCT WHICH GIVES THE RECIPE ITS NAME. PANCETTA BACON WILL DO JUST FINE)
1 SM. CHILLI
SALT 1 PINCH.
125G. GRATED PECORINO
(A HARD SHEEP'S CHEESE WITH A "PEPPERY" TASTE)
SPAGHETTI
400 GR.
THANKS TO OUR FRIEND CLEMENTINA!
STEP 1. FRY THE BACON IN THE OIL, THEN ADD THE WINE, TOMATOES, CHILLI AND SALT TO TASTE.
STEP 2. STIR AND SIMMER ON LOW HEAT UNTIL SAUCE IS THICKER AND NO LONGER "WATERY".
STEP 3. MEANWHILE, BOIL A PAN OF WATER AND COOK THE SPAGHETTI.
JUST FOLLOW THE INSTRUCTIONS ON THE PACKET
STEP 4. DRAIN THE SPAGHETTI AND STIR IT INTO THE SAUCE.
ADD GRATED PECORINO AND SERVE!
DELICIOUS
BUON APPETITO

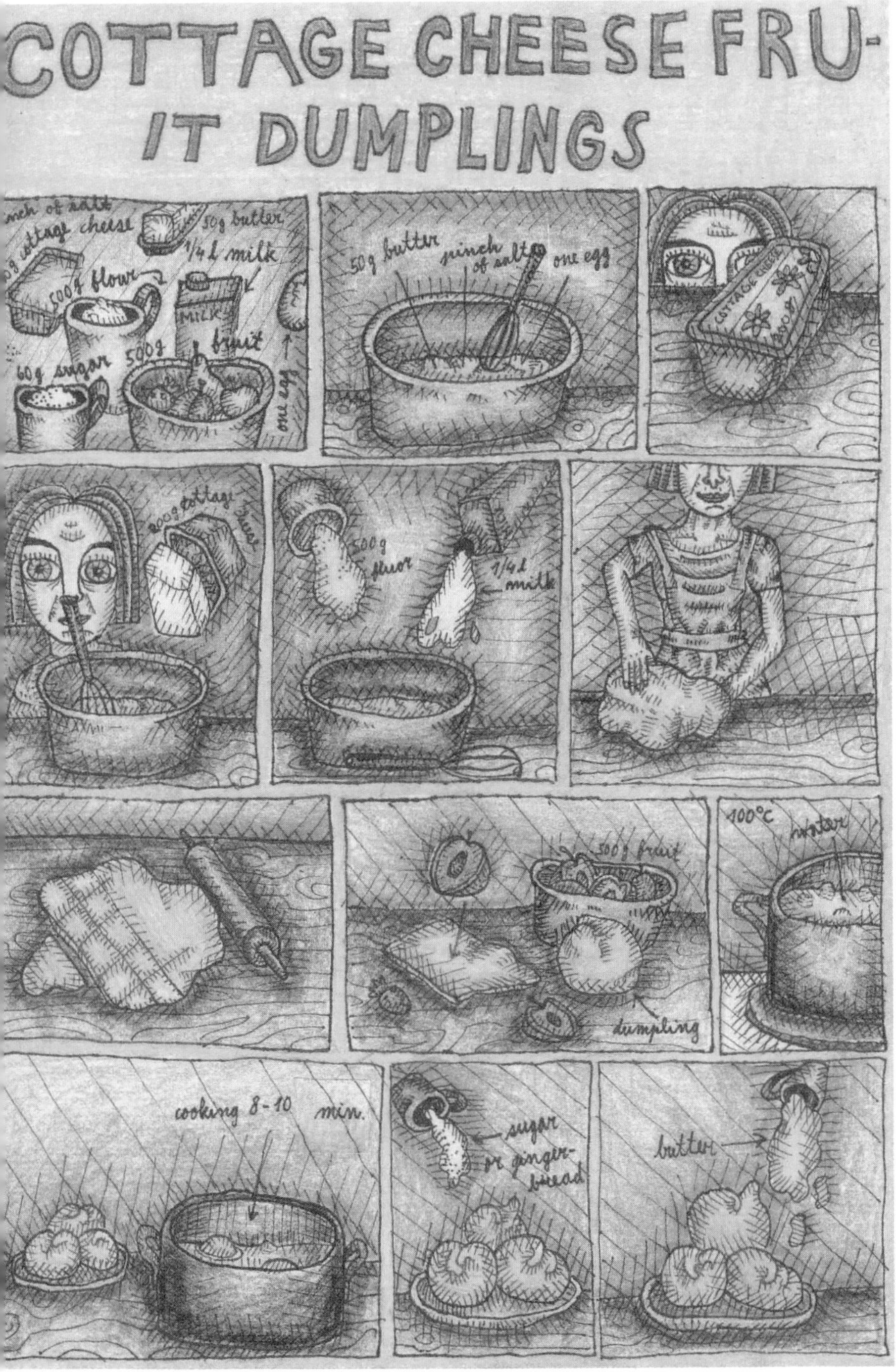
COTTAGE CHEESE FRU-
IT DUMPLINGS
cottage cheese
50g butter
1/4 l milk
500g flour
MILK
fruit
60g sugar
500g
one egg
50g butter
pinch of salt
one egg
COTTAGE CHEESE
500g
500g cottage cheese
500g flour
1/4 l milk
500g fruit
dumpling
100°C
water
cooking 8-10 min.
sugar
or ginger-bread
butter

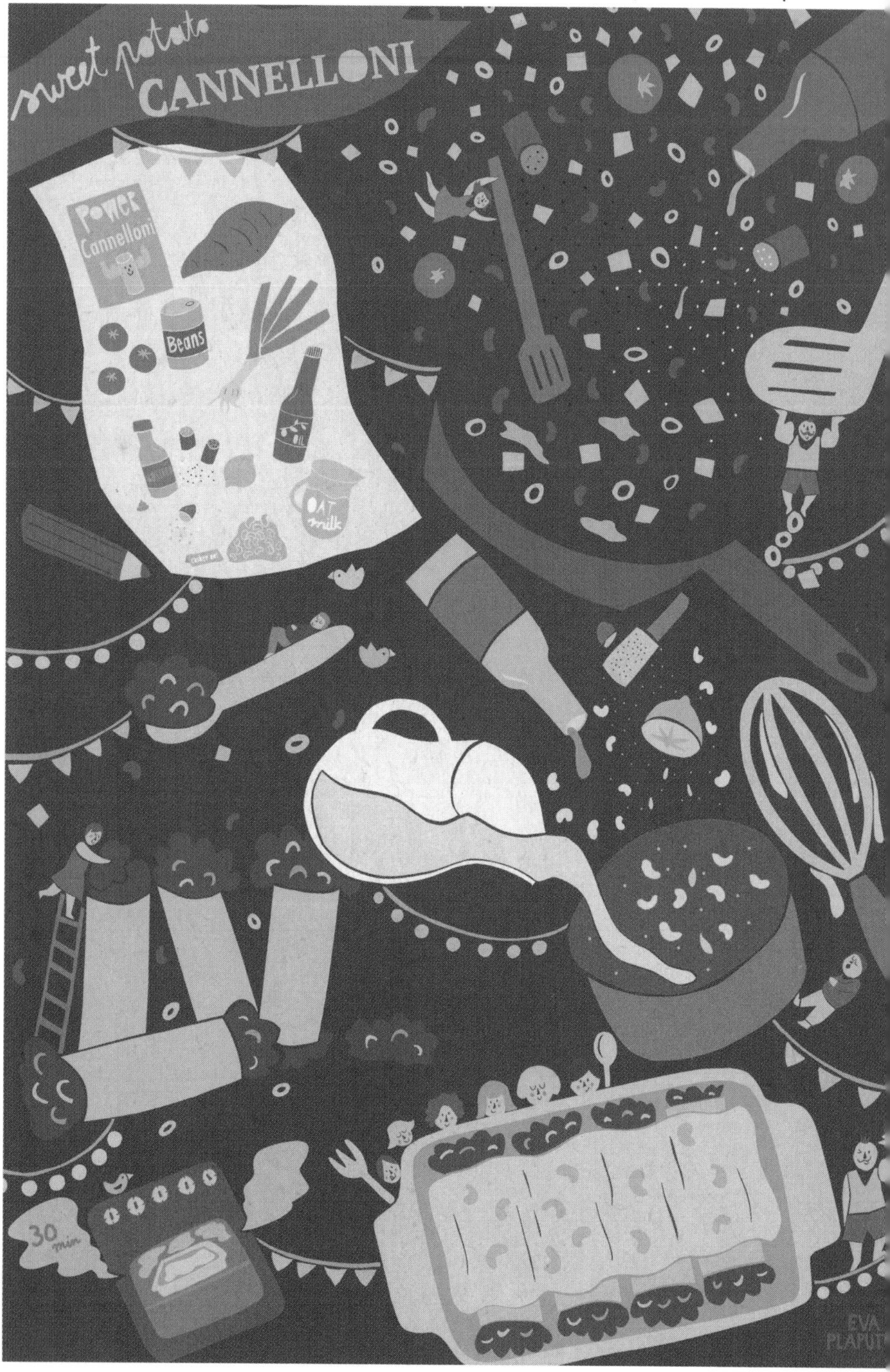
sweet potato
CANNELLONI
Power
Cannelloni
Beans
OIL
OAT
milk
30
min
EVA

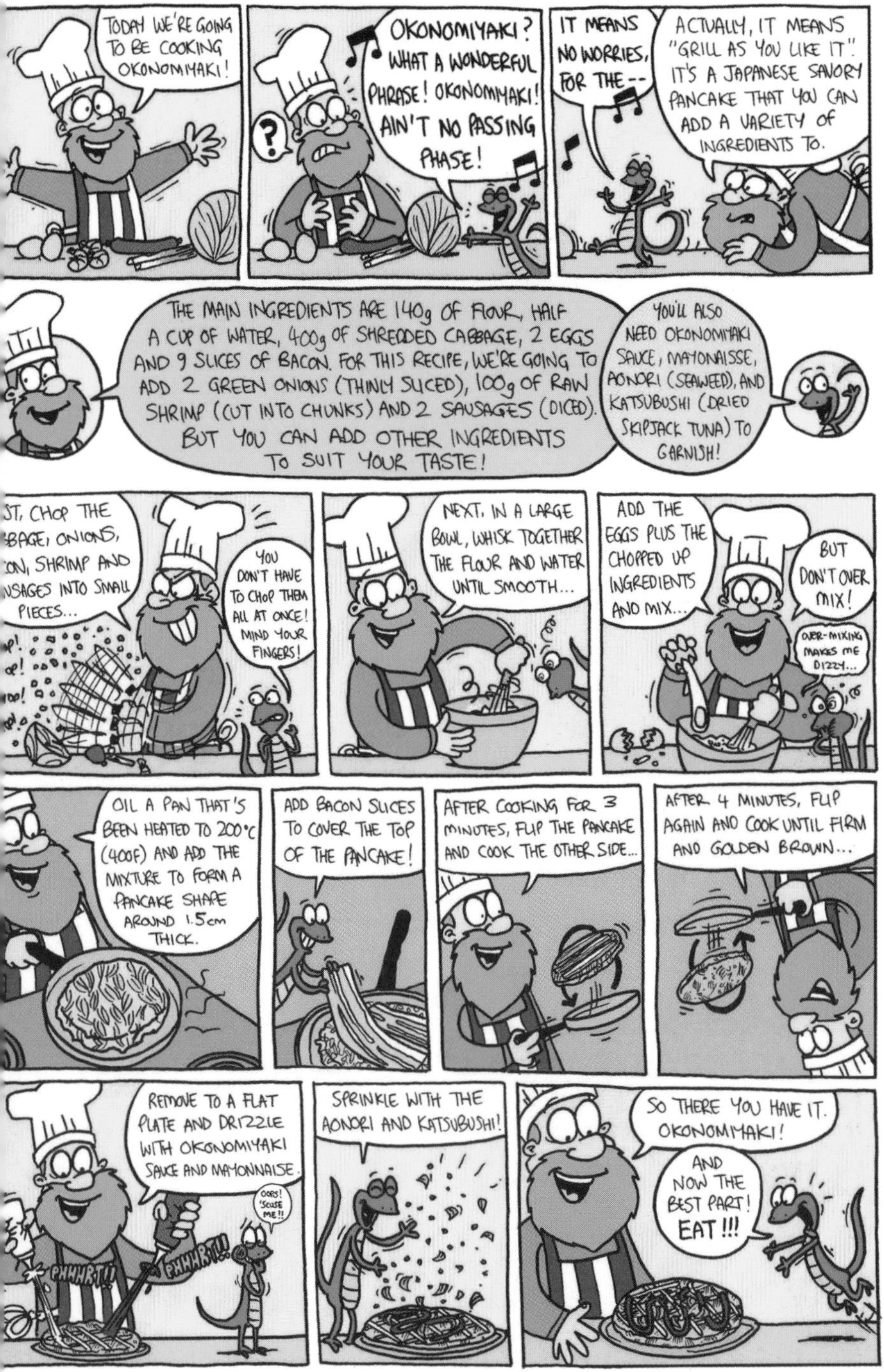
TODAY WE'RE GOING TO BE COOKING OKONOMIYAKI!
OKONOMIYAKI? WHAT A WONDERFUL PHRASE! OKONOMIYAKI! AIN'T NO PASSING PHASE!
?
IT MEANS NO WORRIES, FOR THE --
ACTUALLY, IT MEANS "GRILL AS YOU LIKE IT". IT'S A JAPANESE SAVORY PANCAKE THAT YOU CAN ADD A VARIETY OF INGREDIENTS TO.
THE MAIN INGREDIENTS ARE 140g OF FLOUR, HALF A CUP OF WATER, 400g OF SHREDDED CABBAGE, 2 EGGS AND 9 SLICES OF BACON. FOR THIS RECIPE, WE'RE GOING TO ADD 2 GREEN ONIONS (THINLY SLICED), 100g OF RAW SHRIMP (CUT INTO CHUNKS) AND 2 SAUSAGES (DICED). BUT YOU CAN ADD OTHER INGREDIENTS TO SUIT YOUR TASTE!
YOU'LL ALSO NEED OKONOMIYAKI SAUCE, MAYONAISSE, AONORI (SEAWEED), AND KATSUBUSHI (DRIED SKIPJACK TUNA) TO GARNISH!
ST, CHOP THE BBAGE, ONIONS, CON, SHRIMP AND USAGES INTO SMALL PIECES...
YOU DON'T HAVE TO CHOP THEM ALL AT ONCE! MIND YOUR FINGERS!
NEXT, IN A LARGE BOWL, WHISK TOGETHER THE FLOUR AND WATER UNTIL SMOOTH...
ADD THE EGGS PLUS THE CHOPPED UP INGREDIENTS AND MIX...
BUT DON'T OVER MIX!
OVER-MIXING MAKES ME DIZZY...
OIL A PAN THAT'S BEEN HEATED TO 200°C (400F) AND ADD THE MIXTURE TO FORM A PANCAKE SHAPE AROUND 1.5cm THICK.
ADD BACON SLICES TO COVER THE TOP OF THE PANCAKE!
AFTER COOKING FOR 3 MINUTES, FLIP THE PANCAKE AND COOK THE OTHER SIDE...
AFTER 4 MINUTES, FLIP AGAIN AND COOK UNTIL FIRM AND GOLDEN BROWN...
REMOVE TO A FLAT PLATE AND DRIZZLE WITH OKONOMIYAKI SAUCE AND MAYONNAISE.
OOPS! 'SCUSE ME!!
PHHHRT!!
PHHHRT!!
SPRINKLE WITH THE AONORI AND KATSUBUSHI!
SO THERE YOU HAVE IT. OKONOMIYAKI!
AND NOW THE BEST PART! EAT!!!

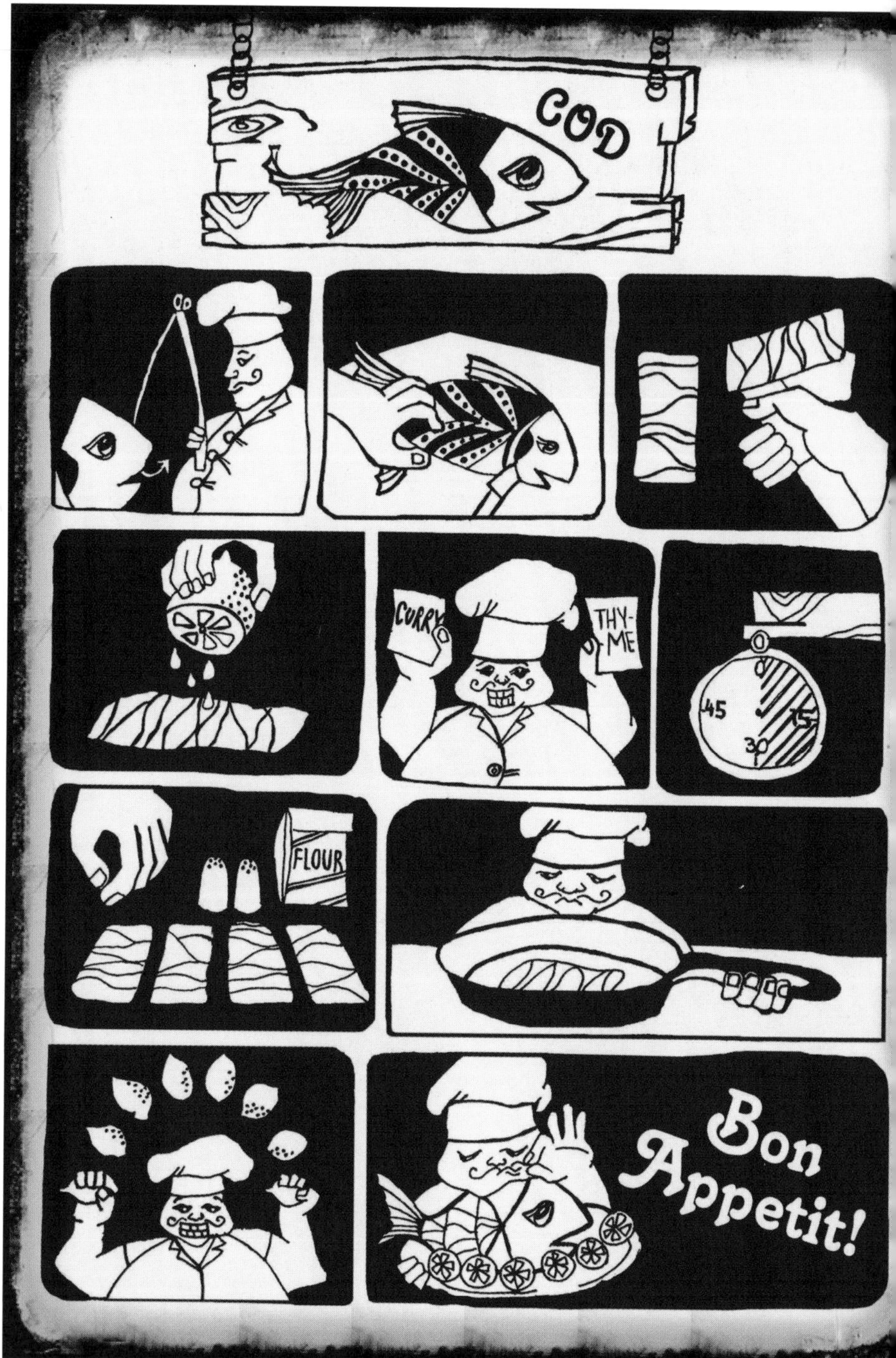
COD
CURRY
THY-
ME
45
15
30
FLOUR
Bon
Appetit!

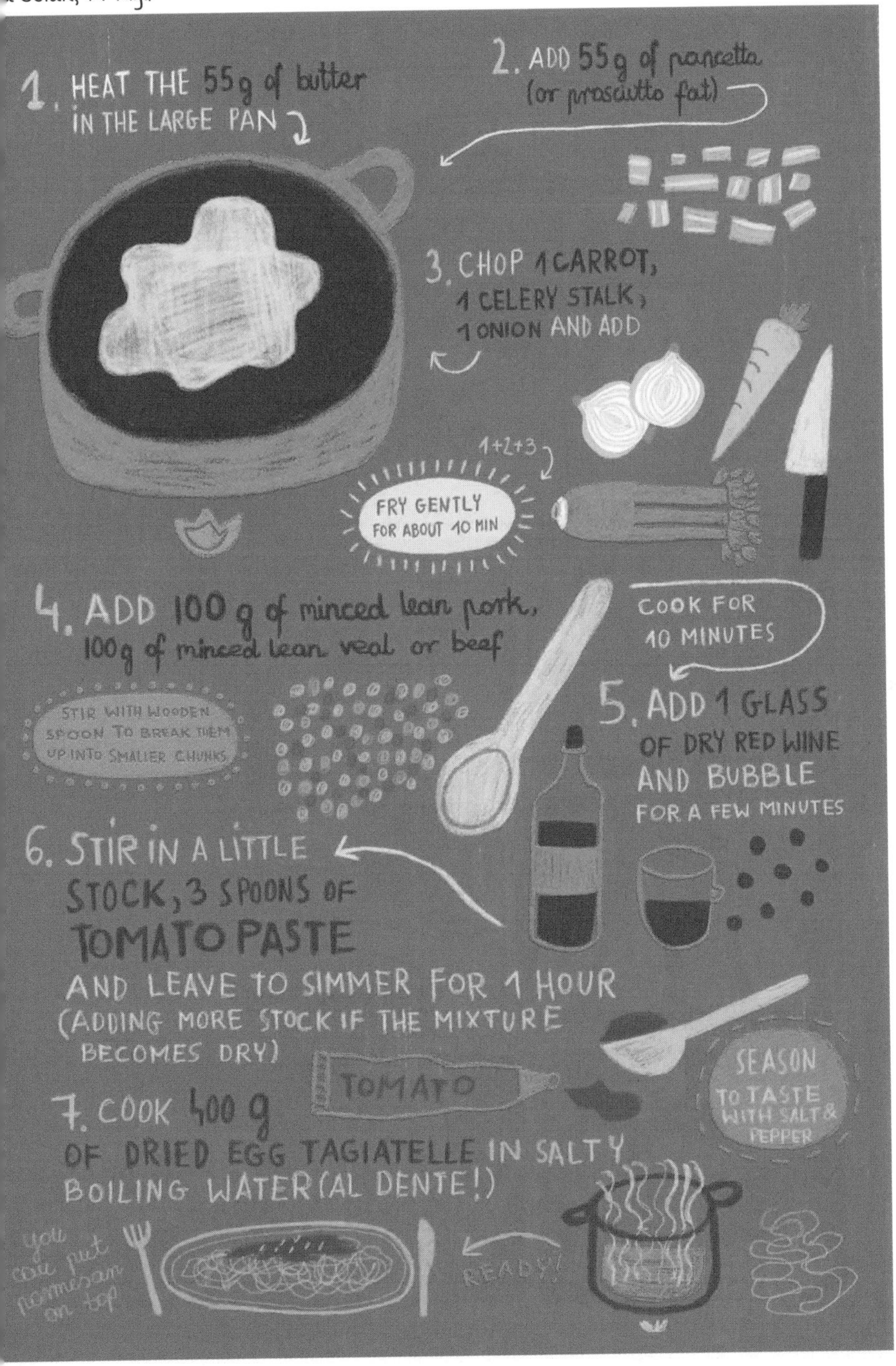
1. HEAT THE 55g of butter IN THE LARGE PAN
2. ADD 55g of pancetta (or prosciutto fat)
3. CHOP 1 CARROT, 1 CELERY STALK, 1 ONION AND ADD
1+2+3
FRY GENTLY FOR ABOUT 10 MIN
4. ADD 100 g of minced lean pork, 100g of minced lean veal or beef
STIR WITH WOODEN SPOON TO BREAK THEM UP INTO SMALLER CHUNKS
COOK FOR 10 MINUTES
5. ADD 1 GLASS OF DRY RED WINE AND BUBBLE FOR A FEW MINUTES
6. STIR IN A LITTLE STOCK, 3 SPOONS OF TOMATO PASTE AND LEAVE TO SIMMER FOR 1 HOUR (ADDING MORE STOCK IF THE MIXTURE BECOMES DRY)
TOMATO
SEASON TO TASTE WITH SALT & PEPPER
7. COOK 400 g OF DRIED EGG TAGIATELLE IN SALTY BOILING WATER (AL DENTE!)
you can put parmesan on top
READY!

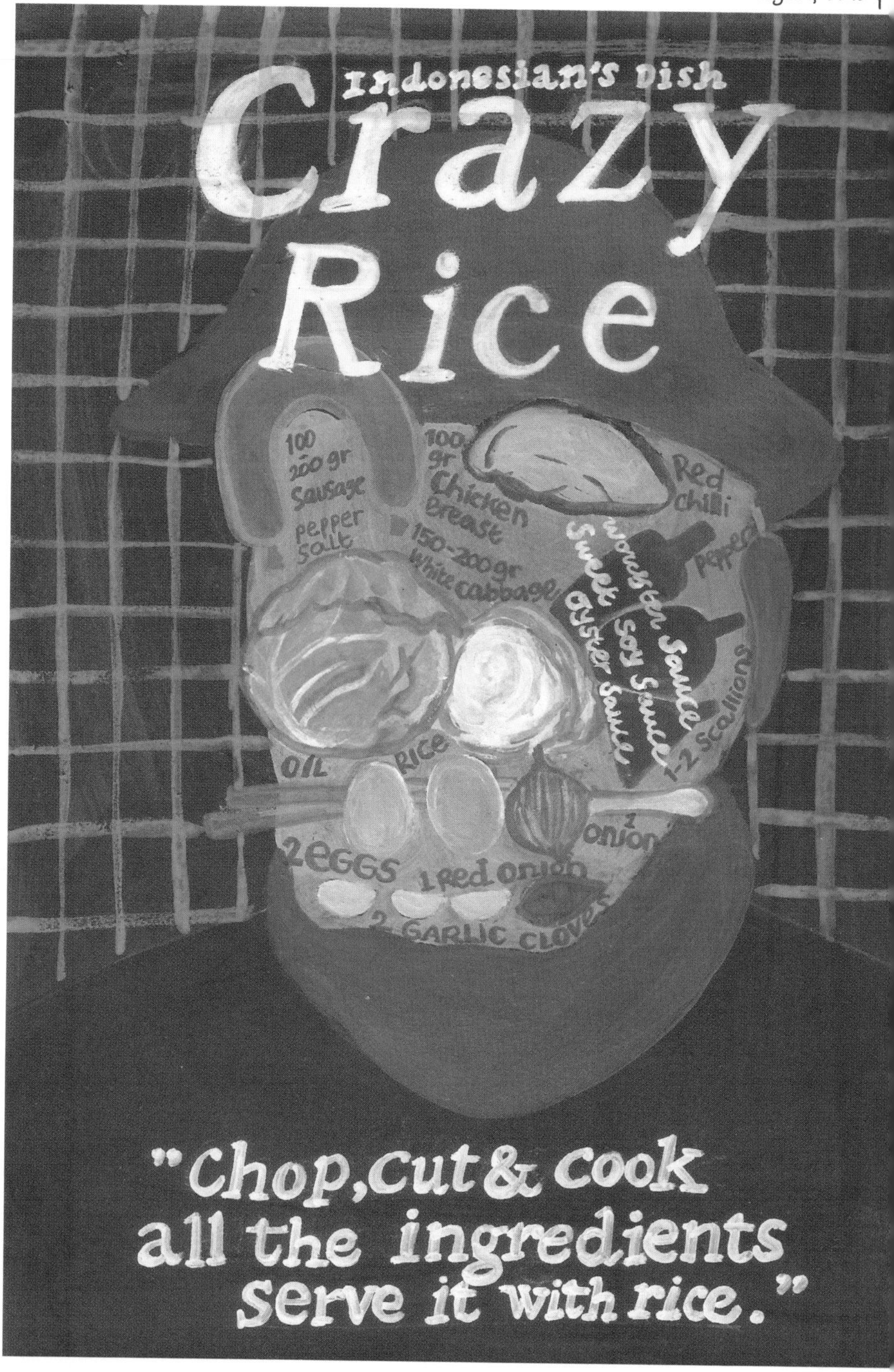
Indonesian's Dish
Crazy Rice
100 - 200 gr Sausage
pepper salt
100 gr Chicken Breast
Red chilli
pepper
150-200 gr White cabbage
Worcester Sauce
Sweet Soy Sauce
Oyster Sauce
1-2 Scallions
OIL
RICE
1 onion
2 EGGS
1 Red onion
2 GARLIC CLOVES
"Chop, Cut & Cook all the ingredients serve it with rice."

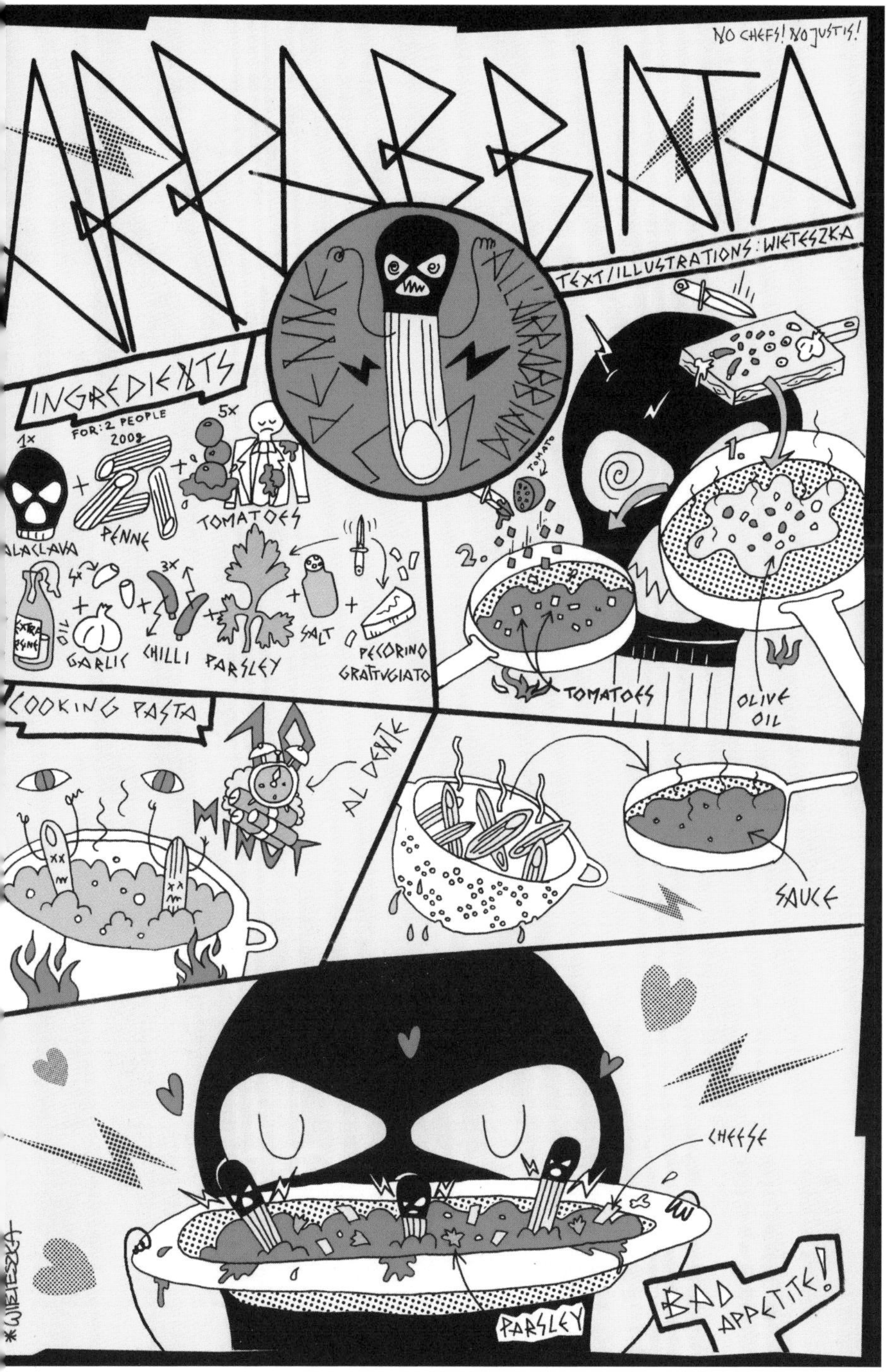
NO CHEFS! NO JUSTIS!
ARRABBIATA
PENNE ALL'ARRABBIATA
TEXT/ILLUSTRATIONS: WIETESZKA
INGREDIENTS
FOR: 2 PEOPLE
1x BALACLAVA
200g PENNE
5x TOMATOES
OIL
GARLIC
3x CHILLI
PARSLEY
SALT
PECORINO GRATTUGIATO
TOMATO
1.
2.
TOMATOES
OLIVE OIL
COOKING PASTA
10 MIN
AL DENTE
SAUCE
CHEESE
PARSLEY
BAD APPETITE!
WIETESZKA

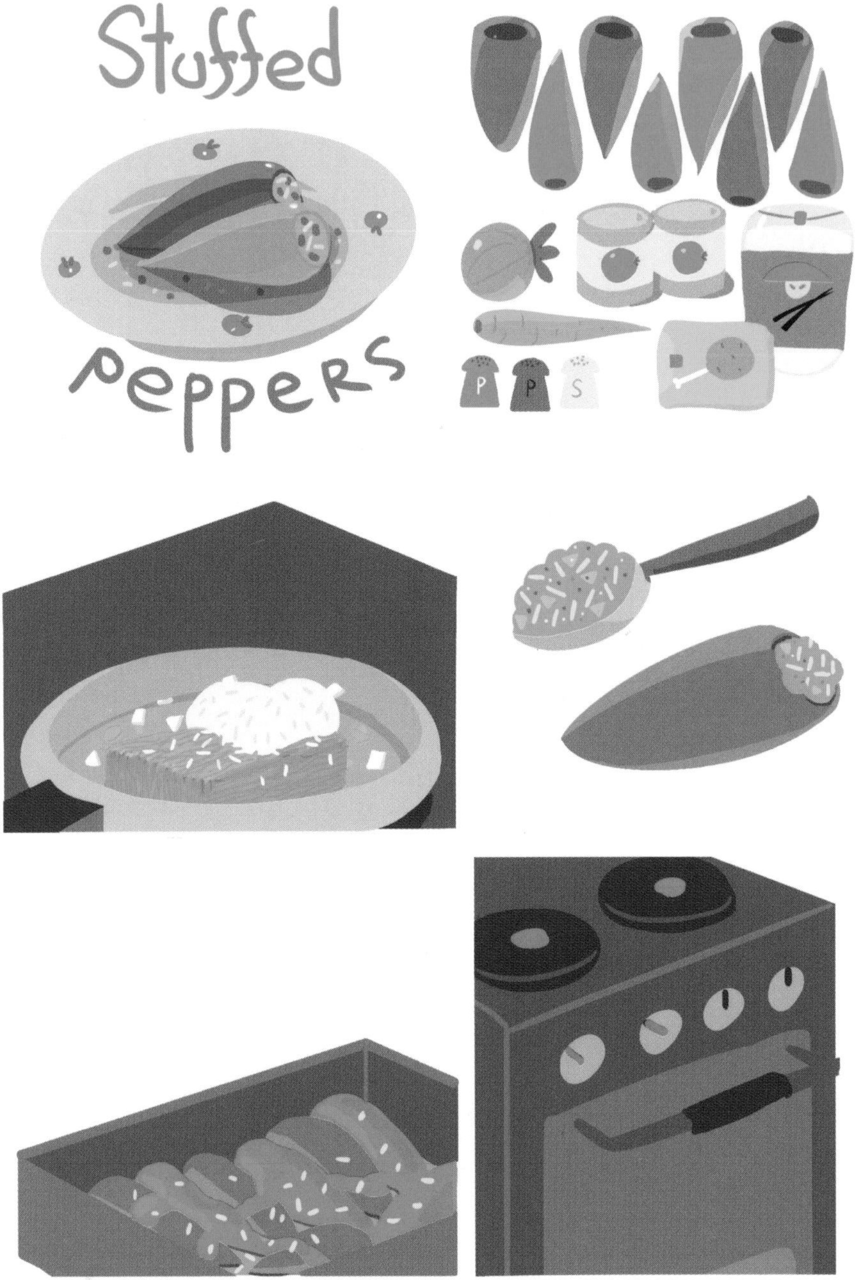
Stuffed
peppers
P
P
S

# Yunhee, Flexible Bulgogi

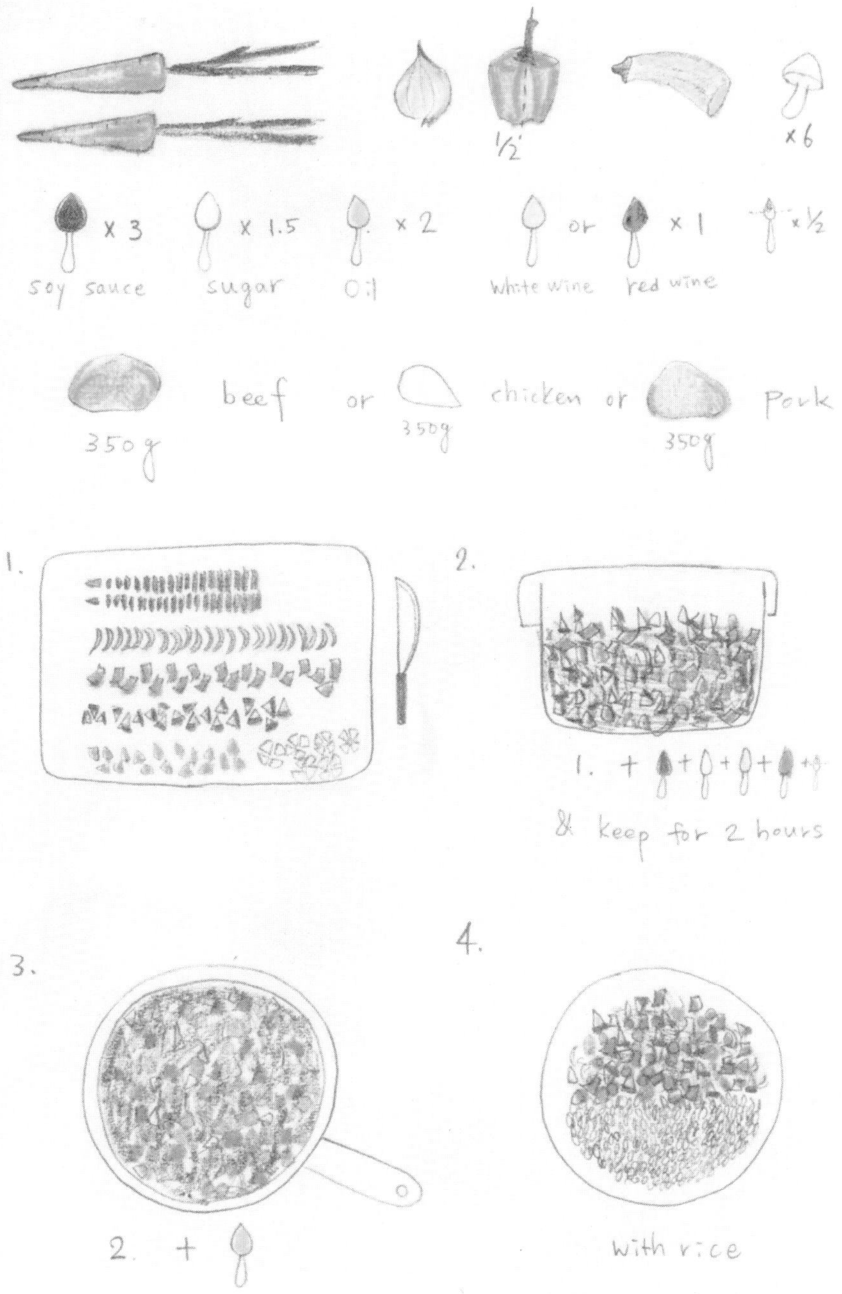

1/2
x 6
x 3
soy sauce
x 1.5
sugar
x 2
Oil
white wine
or
red wine
x 1
x 1/2
350g
beef
or
350g
chicken
or
350g
pork
1.
2.
1. + + + + +
& keep for 2 hours
3.
4.
2. +
with rice

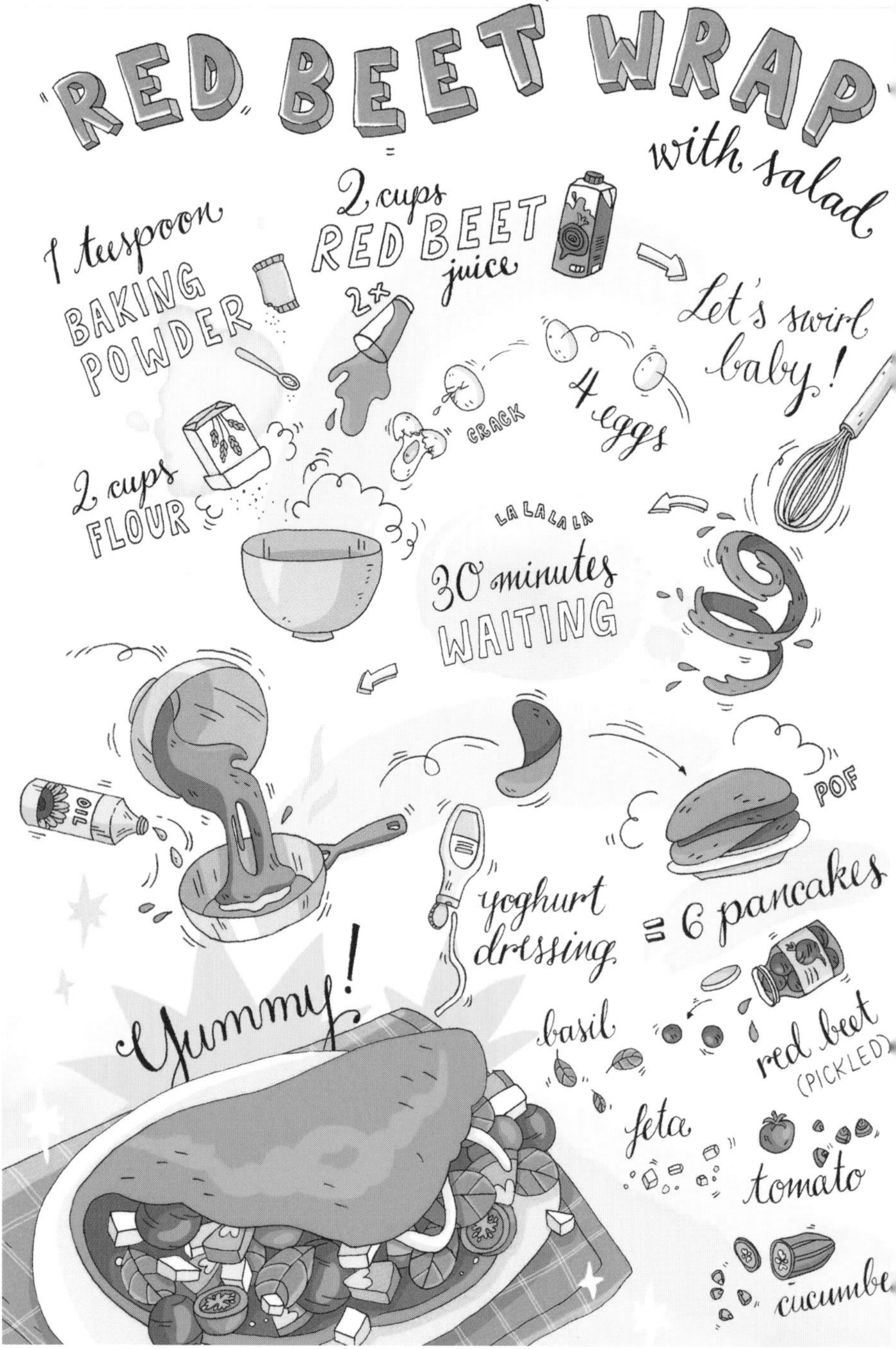
RED BEET WRAP
with salad
1 teespoon
BAKING POWDER
2 cups
RED BEET
juice
2x
Let's swirl baby!
CRACK
4 eggs
2 cups
FLOUR
LA LA LA LA
30 minutes
WAITING
OIL
POF
yoghurt
dressing
= 6 pancakes
Yummy!
basil
red beet
(PICKLED)
feta
tomato
cucumbe

side dishes

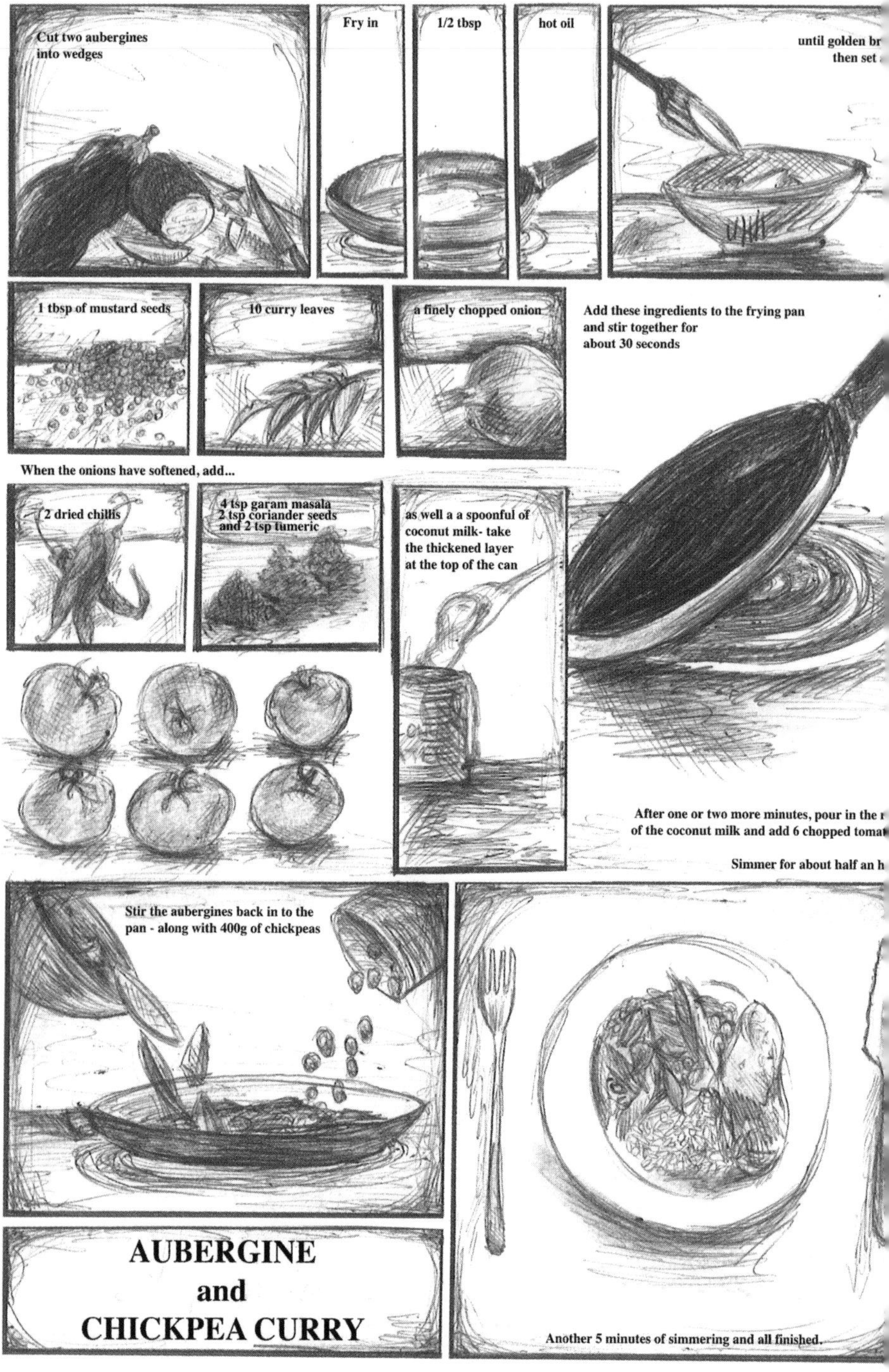
Cut two aubergines into wedges
Fry in
1/2 tbsp
hot oil
until golden br
then set
1 tbsp of mustard seeds
10 curry leaves
a finely chopped onion
Add these ingredients to the frying pan and stir together for about 30 seconds
When the onions have softened, add...
2 dried chillis
4 tsp garam masala 2 tsp coriander seeds and 2 tsp tumeric
as well a a spoonful of coconut milk- take the thickened layer at the top of the can
After one or two more minutes, pour in the
of the coconut milk and add 6 chopped toma
Simmer for about half an h
Stir the aubergines back in to the pan - along with 400g of chickpeas
AUBERGINE
and
CHICKPEA CURRY
Another 5 minutes of simmering and all finished.

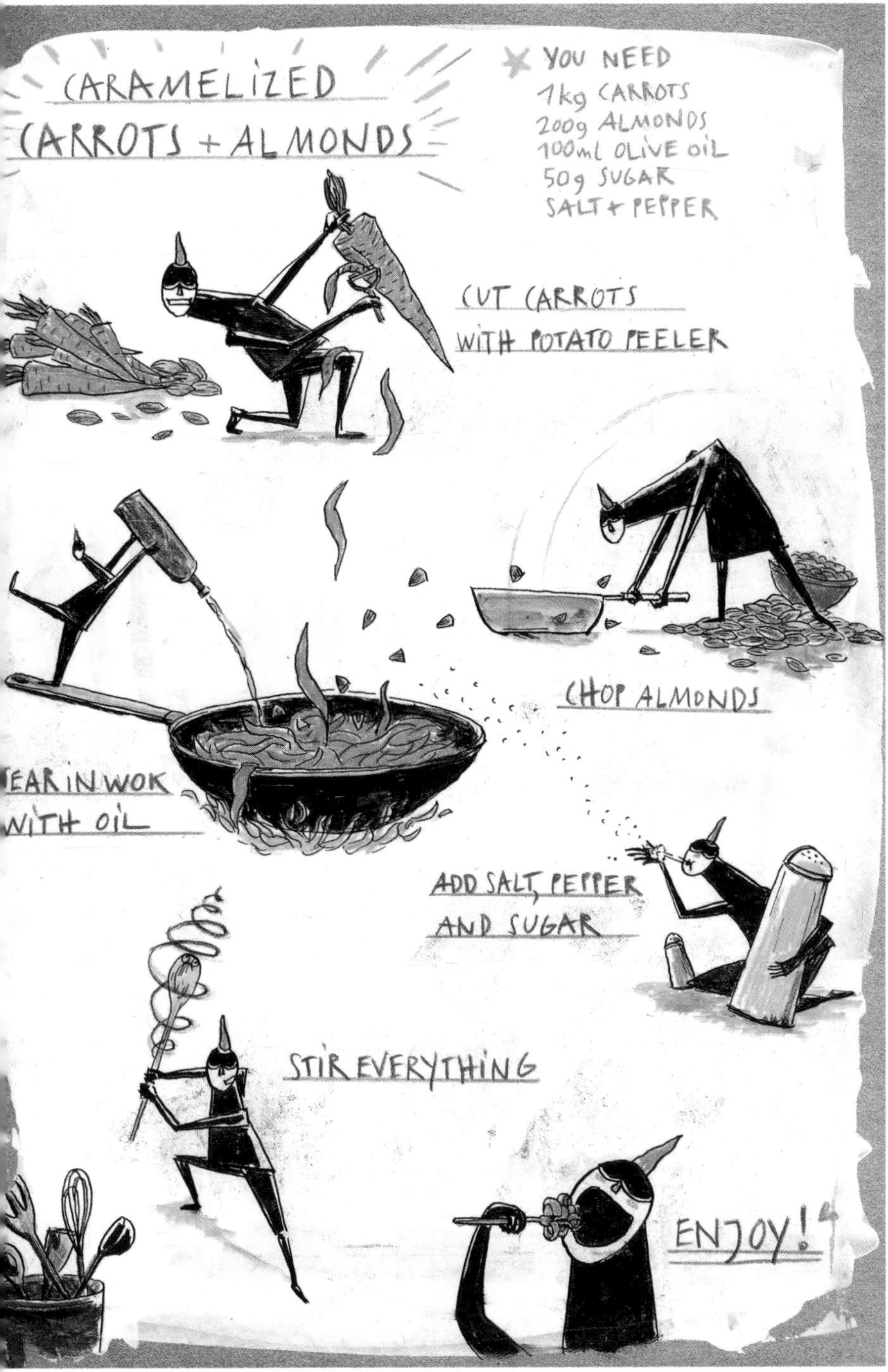
CARAMELIZED
CARROTS + ALMONDS
YOU NEED
1kg CARROTS
200g ALMONDS
100ml OLIVE OIL
50g SUGAR
SALT + PEPPER
CUT CARROTS
WITH POTATO PEELER
CHOP ALMONDS
EAR IN WOK
WITH OIL
ADD SALT, PEPPER
AND SUGAR
STIR EVERYTHING
ENJOY!

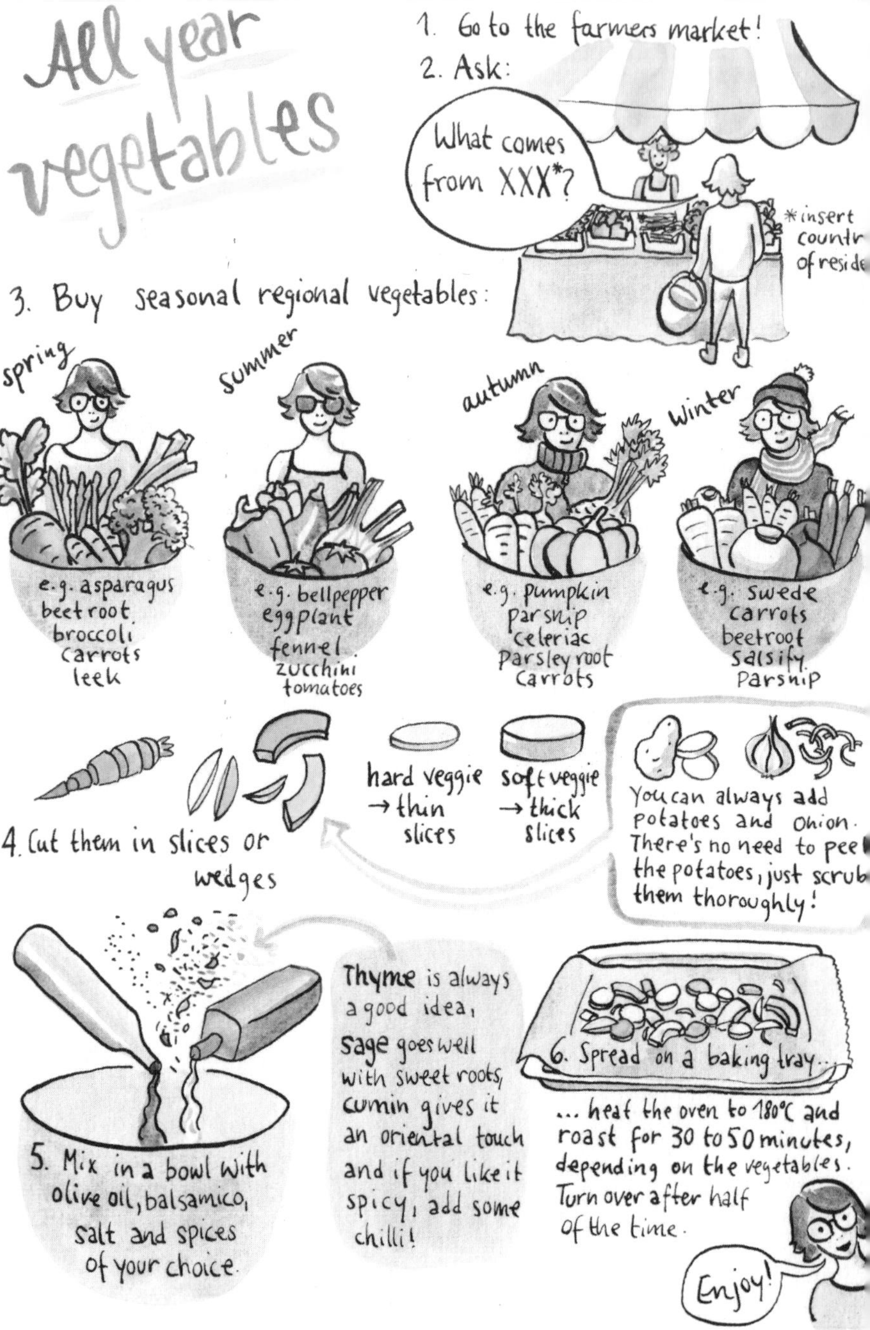
All year vegetables
1. Go to the farmers market!
2. Ask:
What comes from XXX*?
*insert countr of reside
3. Buy seasonal regional vegetables:
spring
e.g. asparagus beetroot broccoli carrots leek
summer
e.g. bellpepper eggplant fennel zucchini tomatoes
autumn
e.g. pumpkin parsnip celeriac parsley root carrots
winter
e.g. swede carrots beetroot salsify parsnip
4. Cut them in slices or wedges
hard veggie → thin slices
soft veggie → thick slices
You can always add potatoes and onion. There's no need to pee the potatoes, just scrub them thoroughly!
5. Mix in a bowl with olive oil, balsamico, salt and spices of your choice.
Thyme is always a good idea, sage goes well with sweet roots, cumin gives it an oriental touch and if you like it spicy, add some chilli!
6. Spread on a baking tray...
... heat the oven to 180°C and roast for 30 to 50 minutes, depending on the vegetables. Turn over after half of the time.
Enjoy!

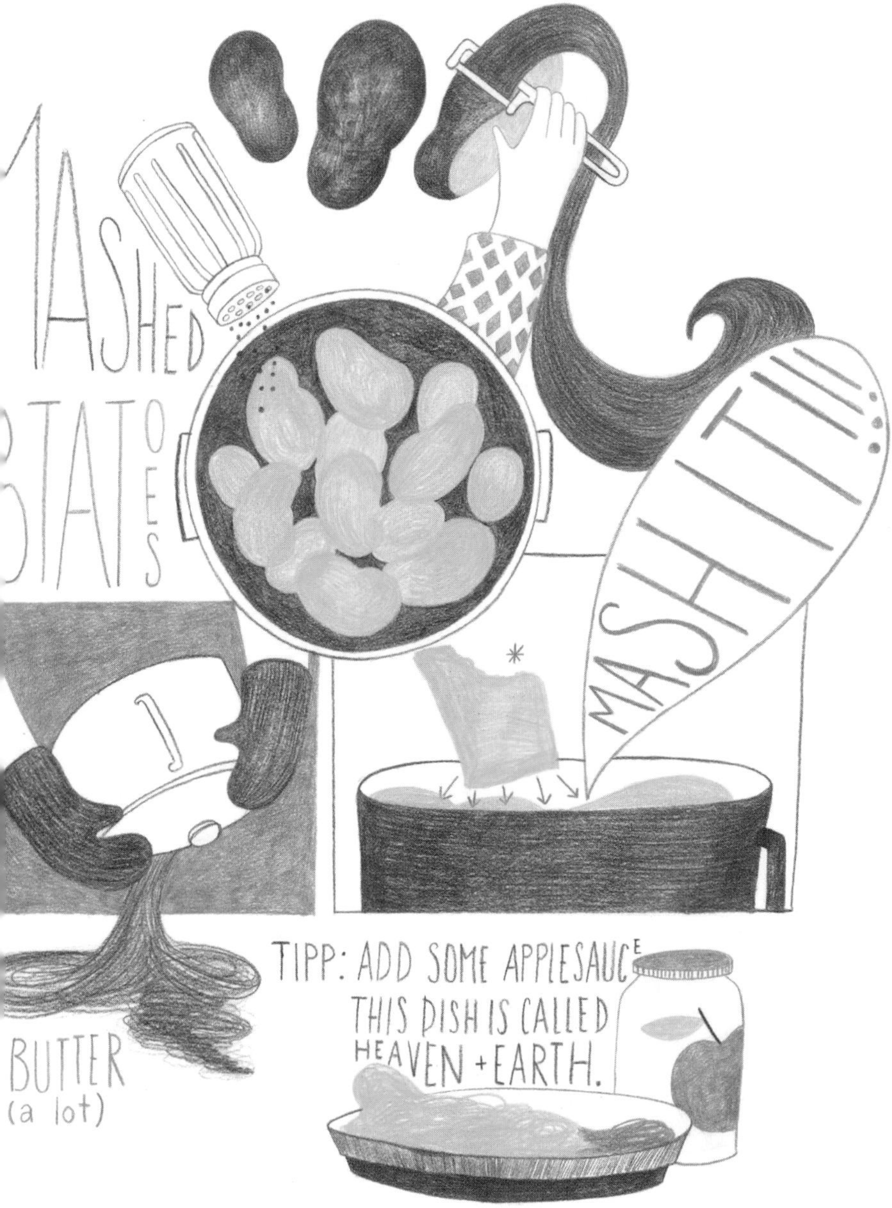
MASHED POTATOES
MASH IT!!!
TIPP: ADD SOME APPLESAUCE
THIS DISH IS CALLED
HEAVEN + EARTH.
BUTTER
(a lot)

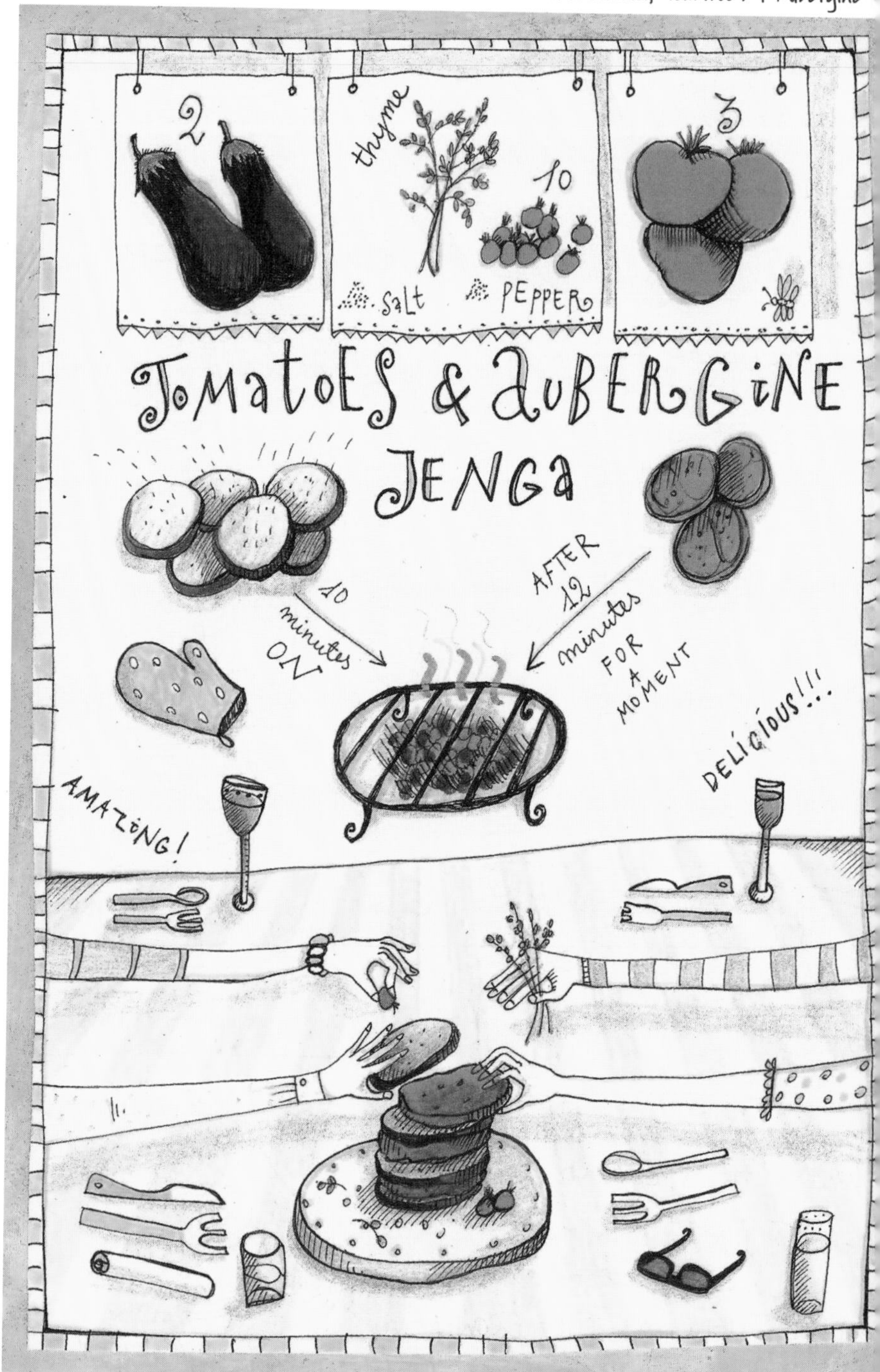
2
thyme
10
3
SALT
PEPPER
TOMATOES & AUBERGINE
JENGA
10 minutes ON
AFTER 12 minutes
FOR A MOMENT
DELICIOUS!!!
AMAZING!

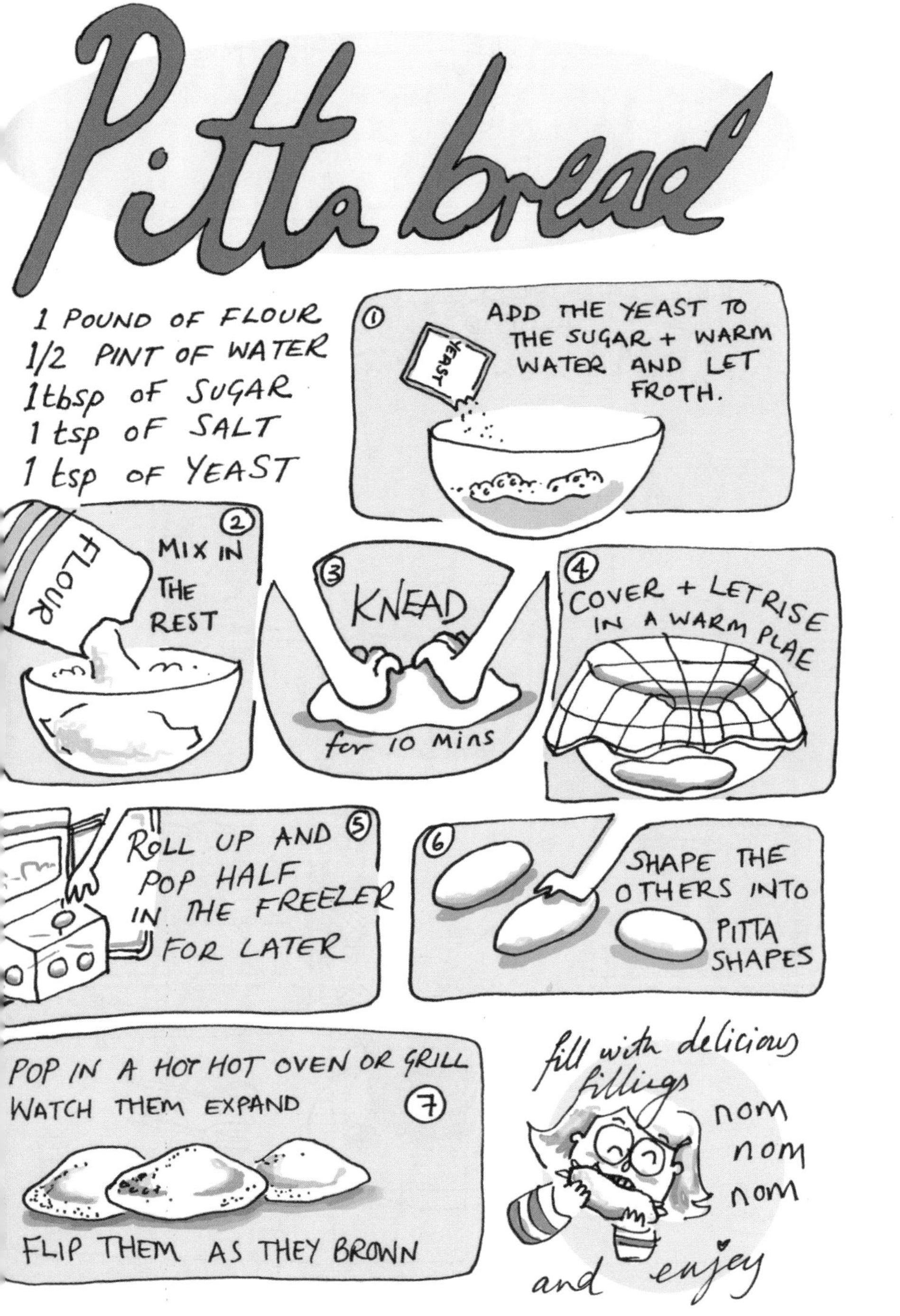
Pitta bread
1 POUND OF FLOUR
1/2 PINT OF WATER
1tbsp OF SUGAR
1 tsp OF SALT
1 tsp OF YEAST
① ADD THE YEAST TO THE SUGAR + WARM WATER AND LET FROTH.
YEAST
② MIX IN THE REST
FLOUR
③ KNEAD for 10 MINS
④ COVER + LET RISE IN A WARM PLAE
ROLL UP AND POP HALF IN THE FREEZER FOR LATER ⑤
⑥ SHAPE THE OTHERS INTO PITTA SHAPES
POP IN A HOT HOT OVEN OR GRILL
WATCH THEM EXPAND ⑦
FLIP THEM AS THEY BROWN
fill with delicious fillings
nom nom nom
and enjoy

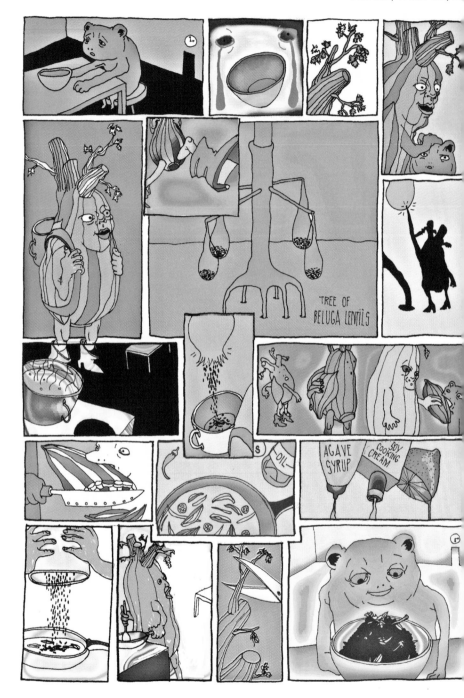

TREE OF
BELUGA LENTILS

AGAVE
SYRUP

OIL

SOY
COOKING
CREAM

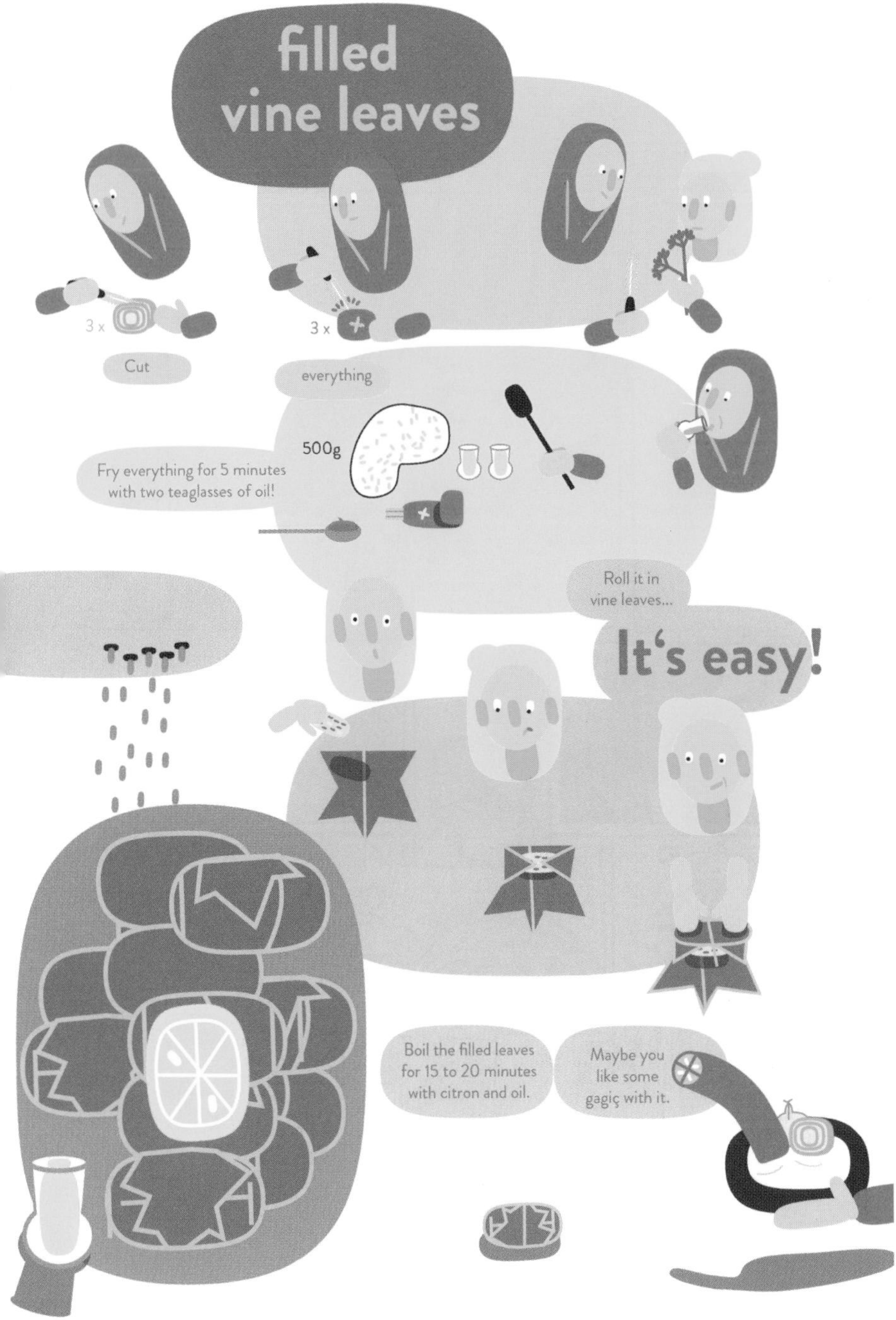
filled
vine leaves
3 x
Cut
3 x
everything
500g
Fry everything for 5 minutes with two teaglasses of oil!
Roll it in vine leaves...
It's easy!
Boil the filled leaves for 15 to 20 minutes with citron and oil.
Maybe you like some gagiç with it.

## Soda bread

Mix the ingredients in order of appearance:

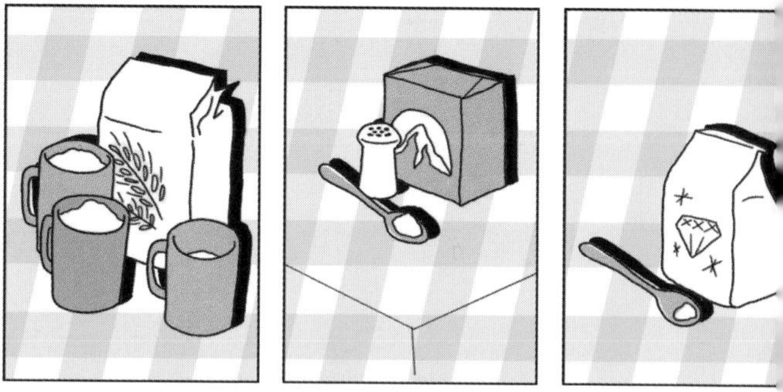

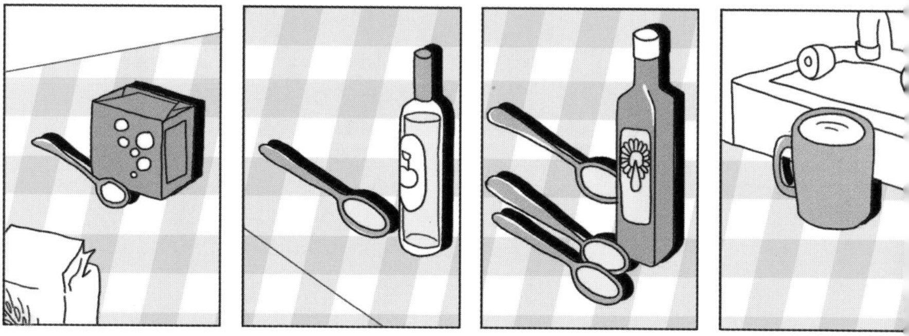

According to your taste, additional ingredients can be added, like the following:

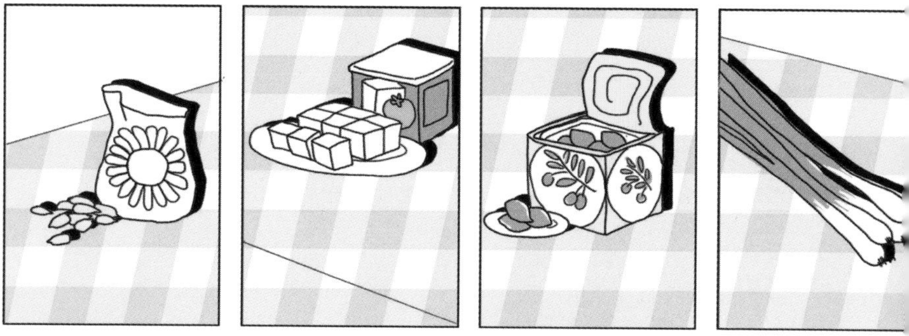

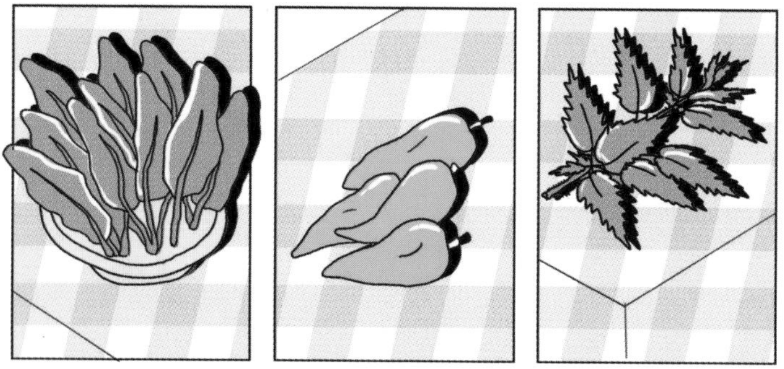

Grease the bottom of a medium size baking dish, powde with a little flour ar put it at 250° in a pre-heated oven for 20 minutes. Enjoy!

drawn by Milena Simeonc

# desserts

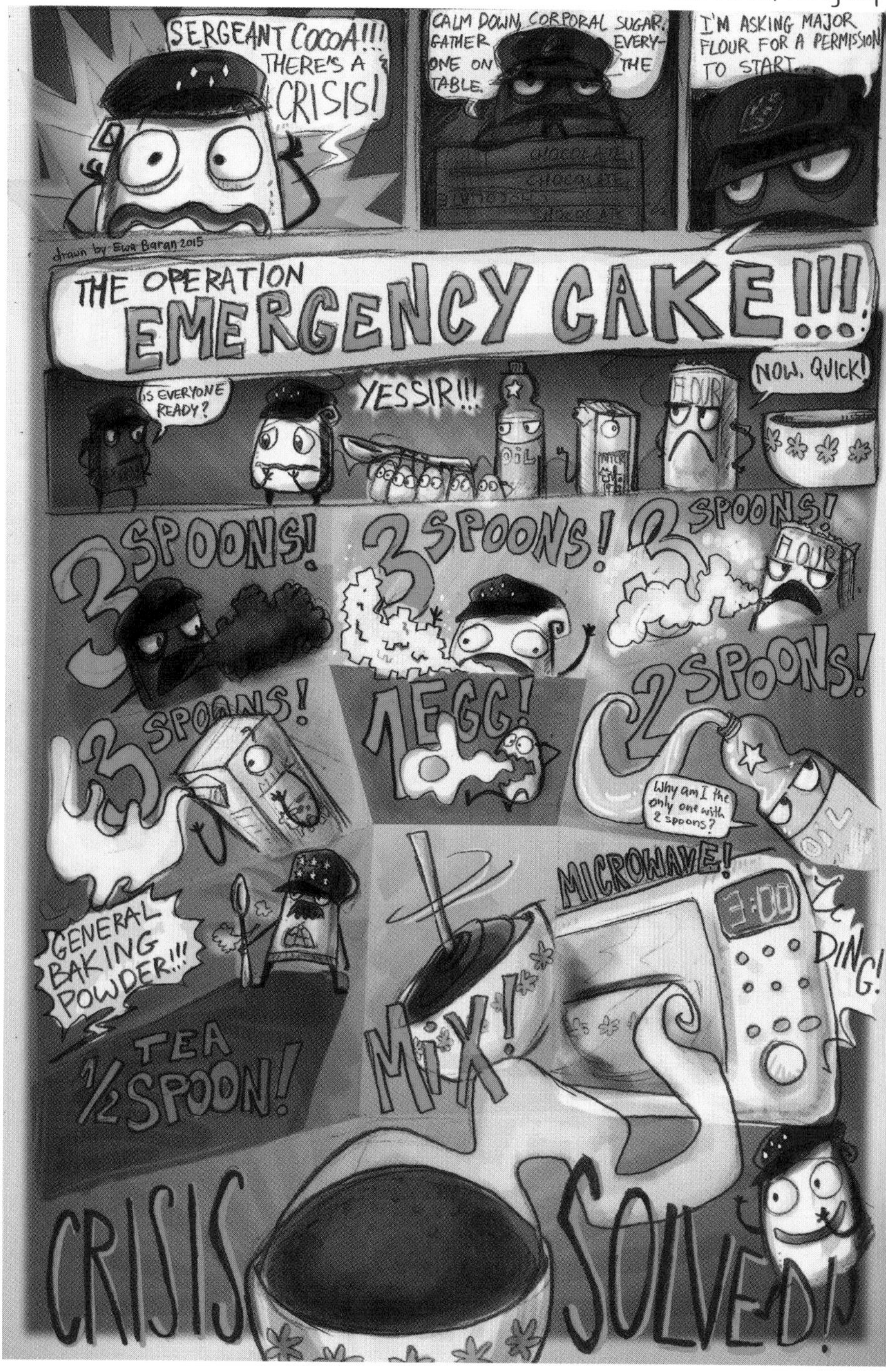
SERGEANT COCOA!!! THERE'S A CRISIS!
CALM DOWN, CORPORAL SUGAR. GATHER EVERYONE ON THE TABLE.
CHOCOLATE
CHOCOLATE
CHOCOLATE
CHOCOLATE
I'M ASKING MAJOR FLOUR FOR A PERMISSION TO START...
drawn by Ewa Baran 2015
THE OPERATION EMERGENCY CAKE!!!...
IS EVERYONE READY?
YESSIR!!!
OIL
FLOUR
NOW, QUICK!
3 SPOONS!
3 SPOONS!
3 SPOONS!
FLOUR
3 SPOONS!
1 EGG!
2 SPOONS!
Why am I the only one with 2 spoons?
OIL
GENERAL BAKING POWDER!!!
TEA 1/2 SPOON!
MIX!
MICROWAVE!
3:00
DING!
CRISIS SOLVED!

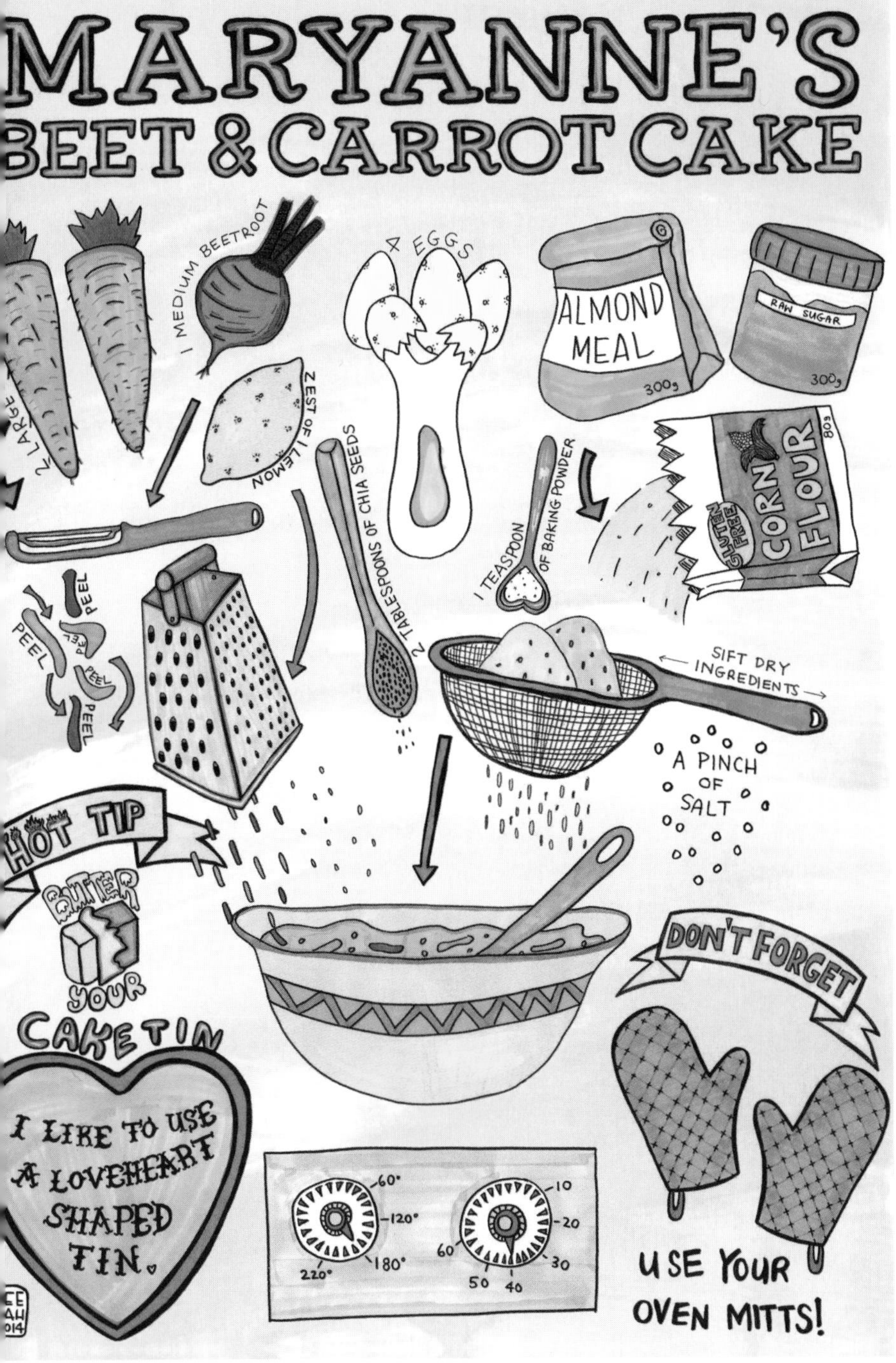
MARYANNE'S
BEET & CARROT CAKE
2 LARGE
1 MEDIUM BEETROOT
ZEST OF LEMON
4 EGGS
ALMOND MEAL
300g
RAW SUGAR
300g
80g
GLUTEN FREE
CORN FLOUR
2 TABLESPOONS OF CHIA SEEDS
1 TEASPOON OF BAKING POWDER
PEEL
PEEL
PEEL
PEEL
PEEL
SIFT DRY INGREDIENTS
A PINCH OF SALT
HOT TIP
BUTTER YOUR CAKETIN
I LIKE TO USE A LOVEHEART SHAPED TIN.
DON'T FORGET
USE YOUR OVEN MITTS!
60°
120°
180°
220°
10
20
30
40
50
60
CE AH 2014

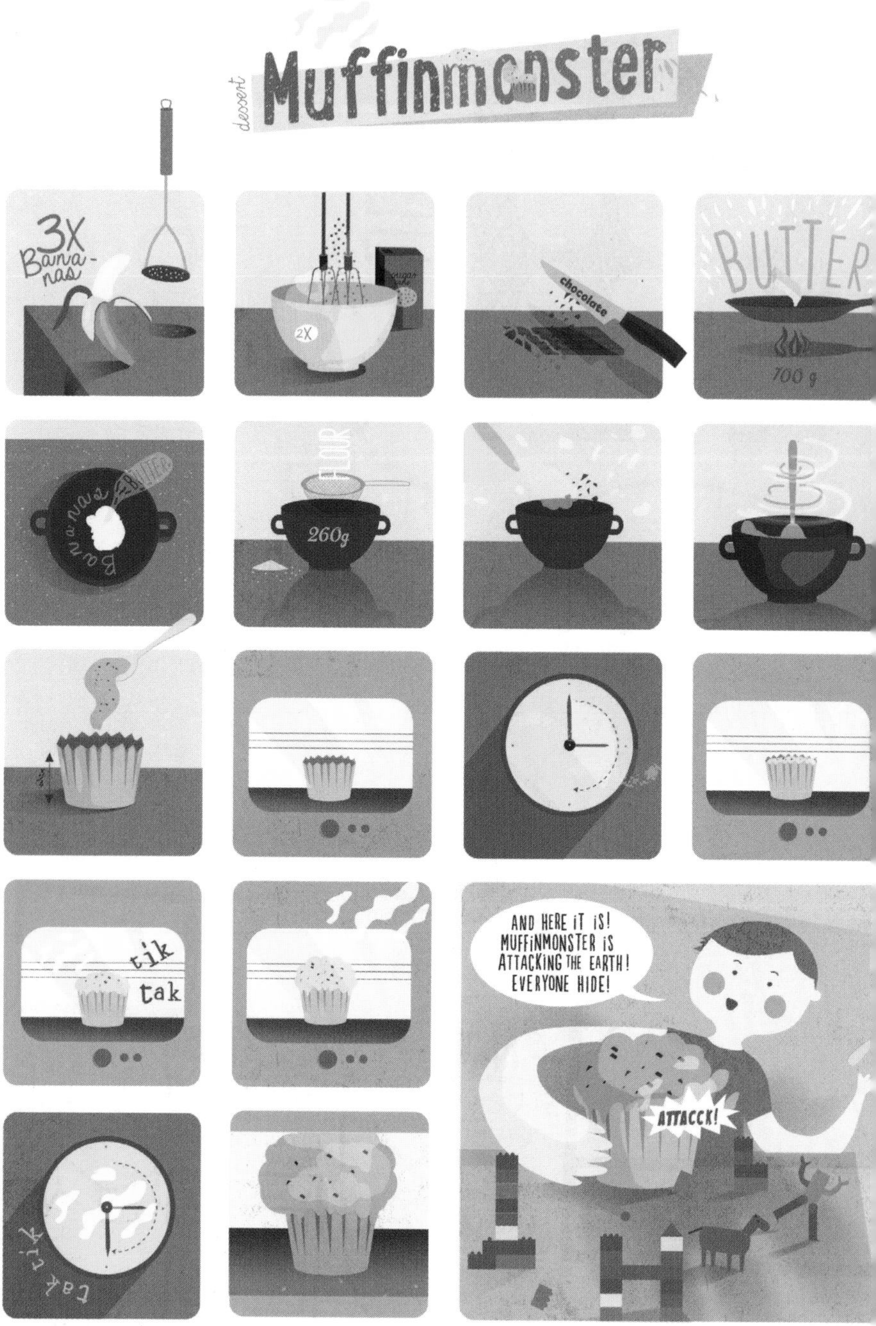
dessert
Muffinmonster
3X
Bana-nas
2X
chocolate
BUTTER
100 g
Bananas
BUTTER
FLOUR
260g
tik
tak
AND HERE iT iS!
MUFFiNMONSTER iS
ATTACKiNG THE EARTH!
EVERYONE HIDE!
ATTACCK!
tik
tak

THE END

# OMA'S CHOCOLATE CAKE

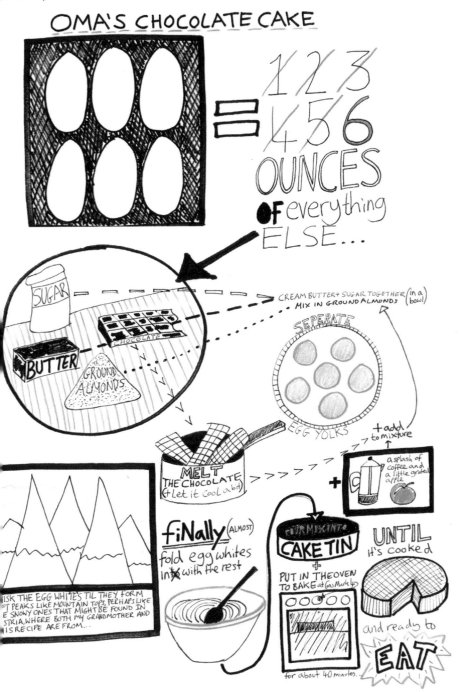

1 2 3 = 4 5 6 OUNCES OF everything ELSE...

SUGAR
BUTTER
CHOCOLATE
GROUND ALMONDS

CREAM BUTTER + SUGAR TOGETHER (in a bowl)
MIX IN GROUND ALMONDS

SEPERATE

EGG YOLKS

+ add to mixture

MELT THE CHOCOLATE (+ let it cool a bit)

a splash of coffee and a little grated apple

fiNally (ALMOST) fold egg whites into with the rest

POUR MIX INTO CAKE TIN + PUT IN THE OVEN TO BAKE at Gas Mark 4

UNTIL it's cooked

ISK THE EGG WHITES TIL THEY FORM T PEAKS LIKE MOUNTAIN TOPS, PERHAPS LIKE E SNOWY ONES THAT MIGHT BE FOUND IN STRIA, WHERE BOTH MY GRANDMOTHER AND IS RECIPE ARE FROM...

for about 40 minutes...

and ready to EAT

75

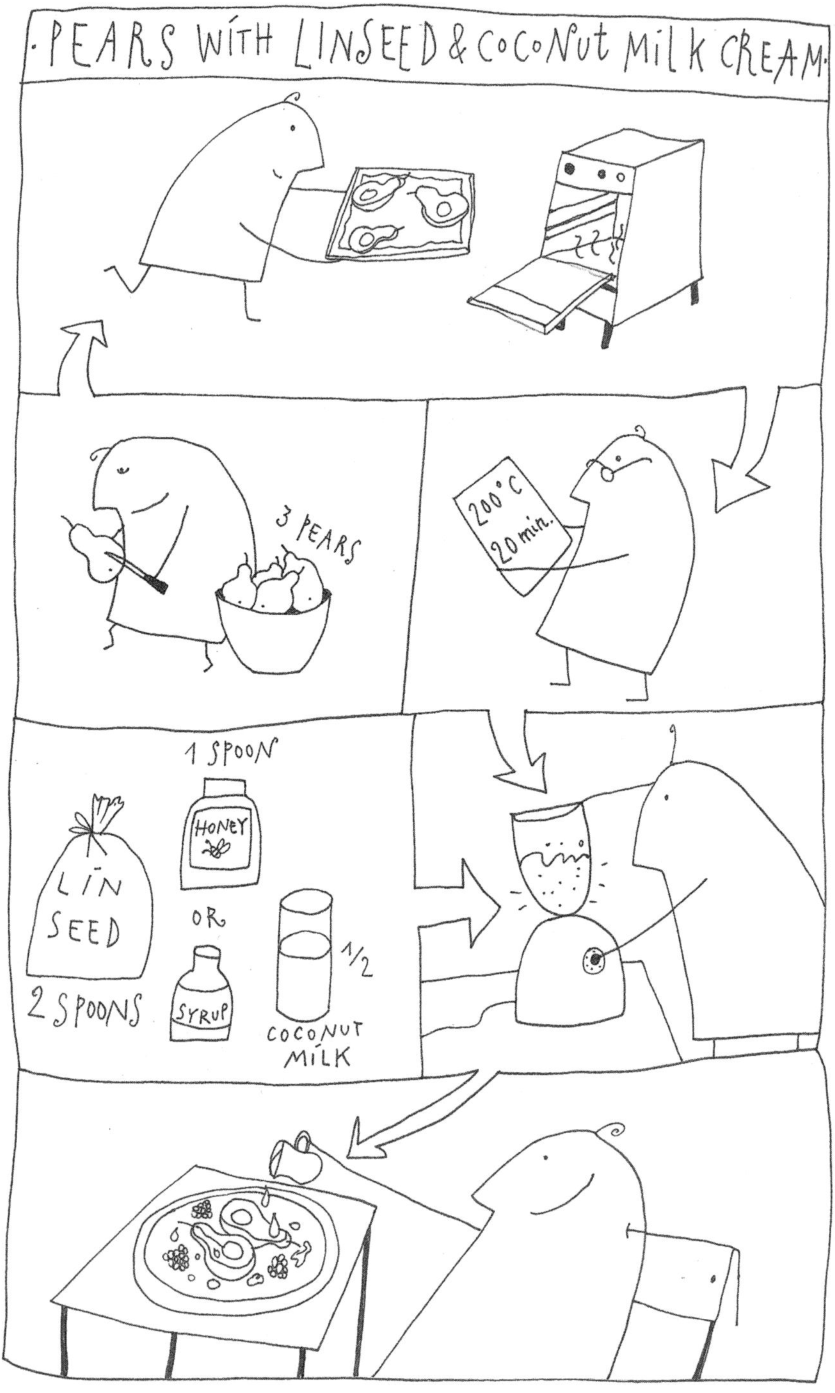
PEARS WITH LINSEED & COCONUT MILK CREAM
3 PEARS
200°C
20 min.
1 SPOON
HONEY
LIN SEED
2 SPOONS
OR
SYRUP
1/2
COCONUT MILK

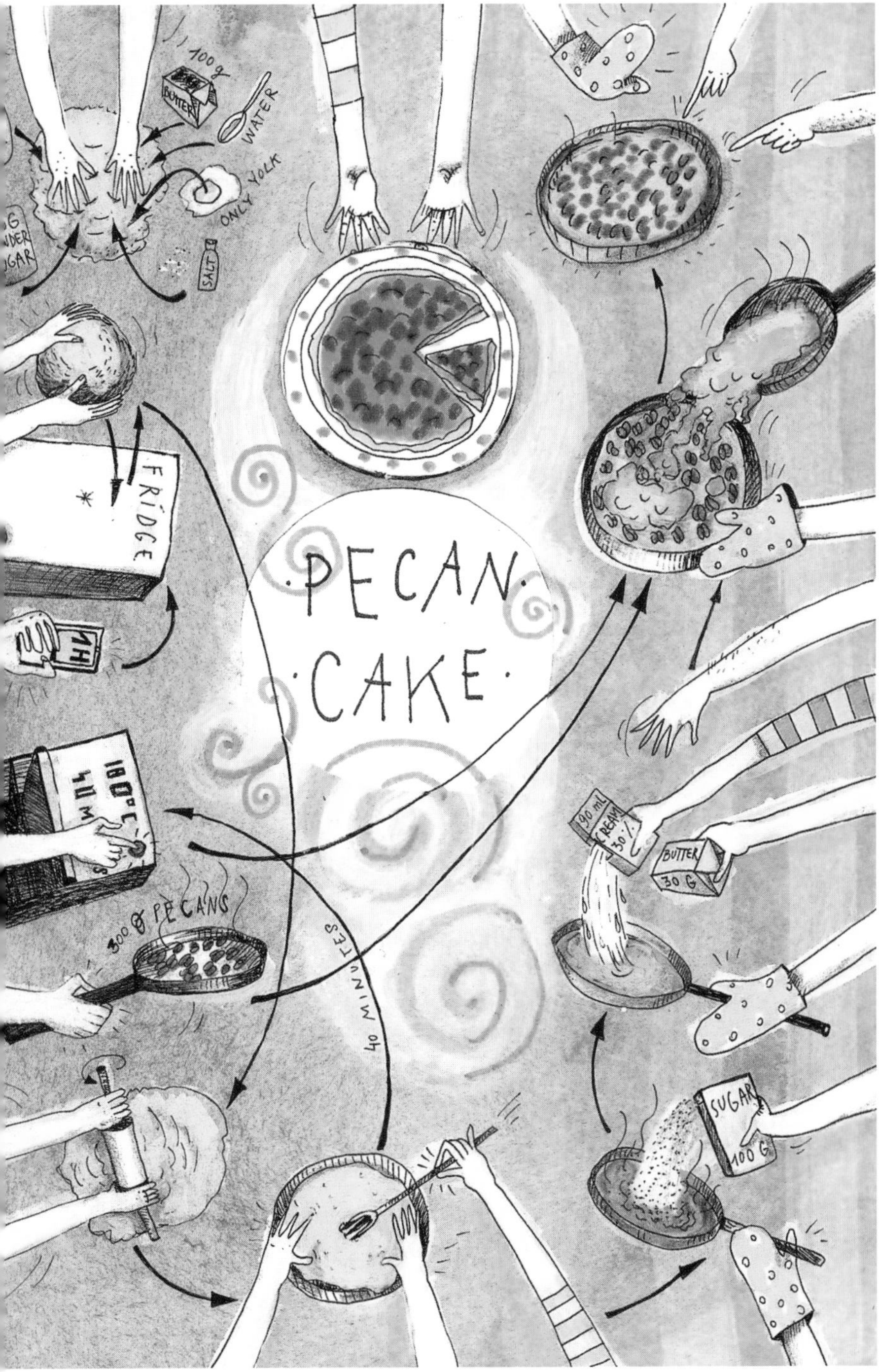
PECAN CAKE
100 g
BUTTER
WATER
ONLY YOLK
SALT
FRIDGE
1H
180°C
40 M
300 g PECANS
40 MINUTES
90 ML
CREAM
30%
BUTTER
30 G
SUGAR
100 G

# Brownie

Collect ingredients:

- 6 eggs
- 300g sugar
- 200g butter
- 100g flour
- 200g chocolate
- 60g walnuts

Melt chocolate & butter.

Whisk the eggs

Mix all ingredients.

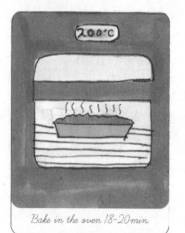

Bake in the oven 18-20min.

Voila!

Enjoy delicious brownie!

BE PARTY PERFECT WITH YOUR OWN TASTY

# ce Cream Comics!

GIVEN SUCCESS AMONG BOTH LARGE AND SMALL

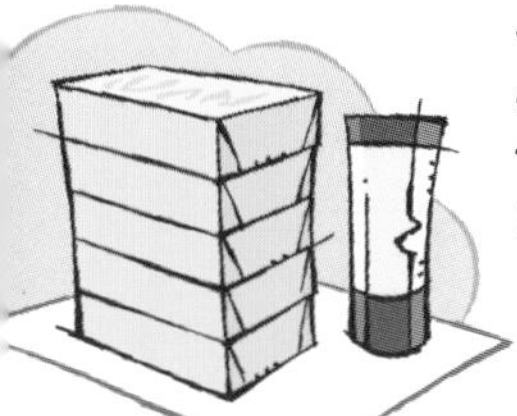

YOU REALLY ONLY NEED THE RIGHT AMOUNT OF STANDARD VANILLA ICE CREAM PACKAGES PLUS A TUBE OF LIQUORICE SAUCE. CUT THE ICE CREAM INTO "PANELS" AND START CREATING!

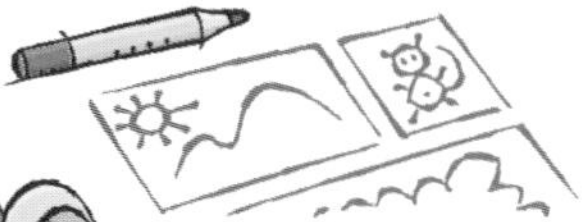

NT MORE LUXURY? USE OTHER UCES – TOFFEE, RASPBERRY, OCOLATE – AND MAYBE JAM, RINKLES, SEEDS, SPICES ETC. ERE ARE ALSO DECORATION LY AND ICING IN DIFFE- NT COLORS.

SKETCH ON PAPER FIRST – PREFERABLY THE RIGHT SIZE – IF YOU DON'T LIKE TO IMPROVISE.

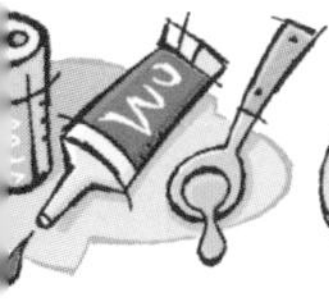

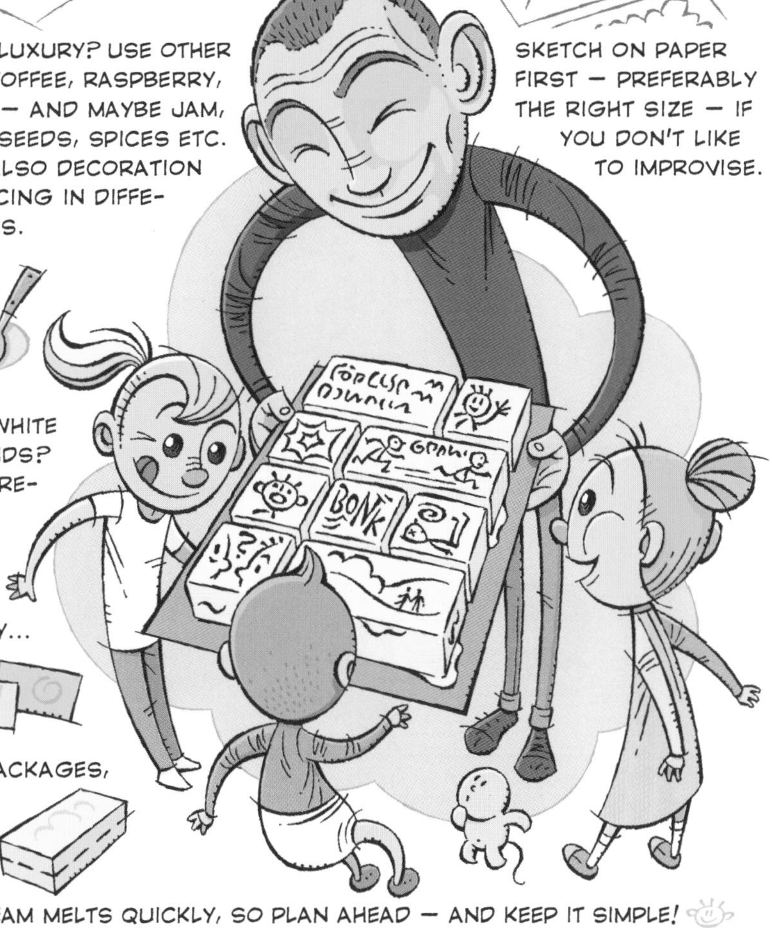
BONK

N'T LIKE WHITE CKGROUNDS? EN TRY "PRE- LOURED" CREAM PEAR, LON, RAWBERRY...

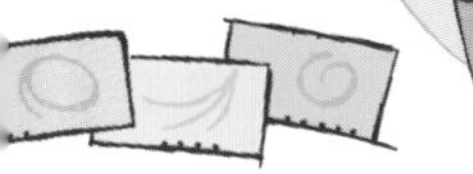

ICE THE PACKAGES, UBLE THE ORY.

S. ICE CREAM MELTS QUICKLY, SO PLAN AHEAD – AND KEEP IT SIMPLE!

## "KOGIEL-MOGIEL"

STIR 4 TEASPOONS OF SUGAR WITH 2 EGG YOLKS

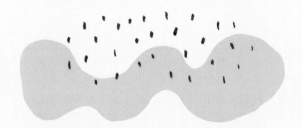

THEN ADD 2 TABLESPOONS OF COCOA

KEEP STIRRING TILL IT'S NICE AND SMOOTH. YUM!

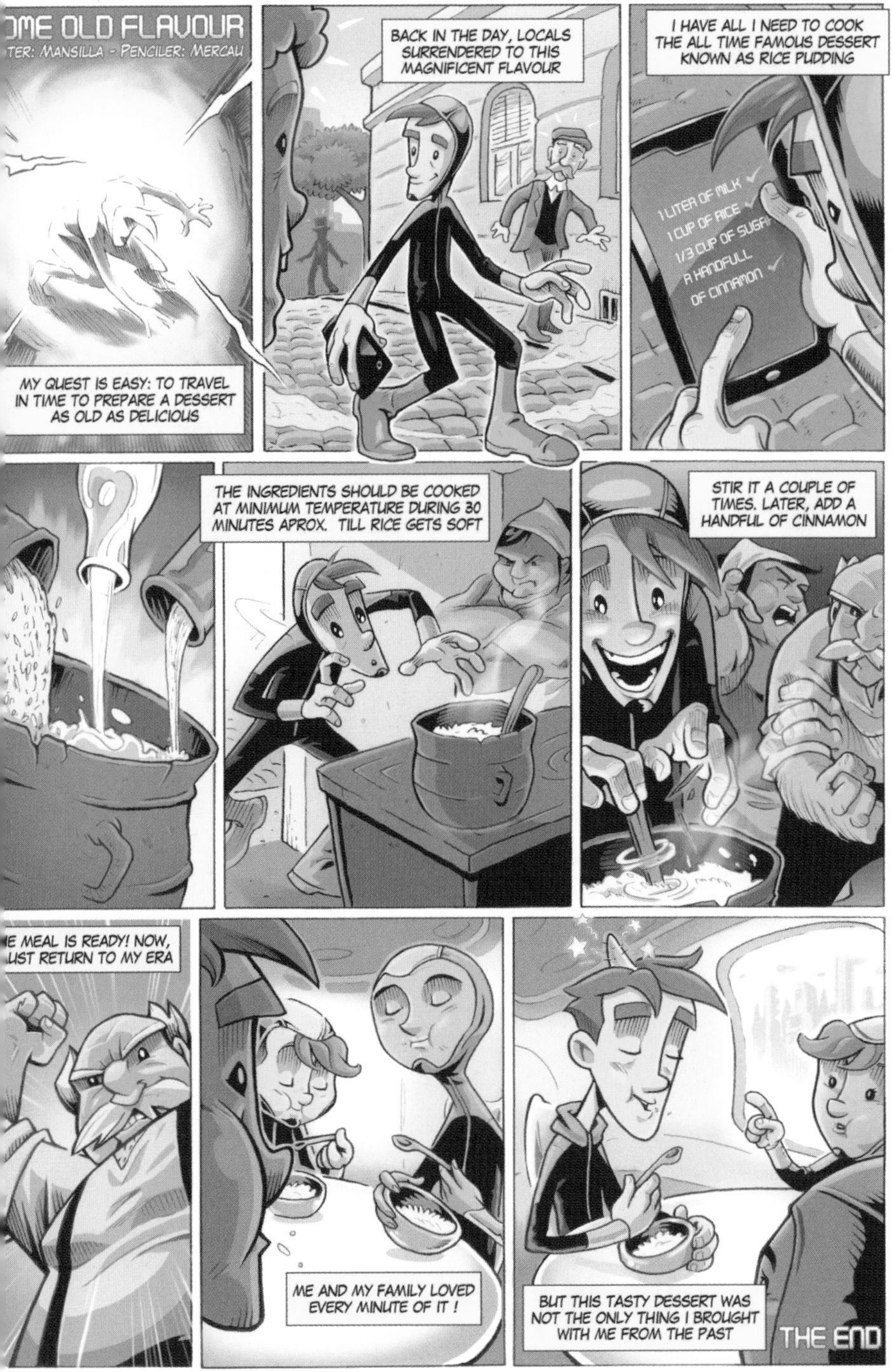
OME OLD FLAVOUR
TER: MANSILLA - PENCILER: MERCAU
MY QUEST IS EASY: TO TRAVEL IN TIME TO PREPARE A DESSERT AS OLD AS DELICIOUS
BACK IN THE DAY, LOCALS SURRENDERED TO THIS MAGNIFICENT FLAVOUR
I HAVE ALL I NEED TO COOK THE ALL TIME FAMOUS DESSERT KNOWN AS RICE PUDDING
1 LITER OF MILK
1 CUP OF RICE
1/3 CUP OF SUGA
A HANDFULL OF CINNAMON
THE INGREDIENTS SHOULD BE COOKED AT MINIMUM TEMPERATURE DURING 30 MINUTES APROX. TILL RICE GETS SOFT
STIR IT A COUPLE OF TIMES. LATER, ADD A HANDFUL OF CINNAMON
E MEAL IS READY! NOW, UST RETURN TO MY ERA
ME AND MY FAMILY LOVED EVERY MINUTE OF IT !
BUT THIS TASTY DESSERT WAS NOT THE ONLY THING I BROUGHT WITH ME FROM THE PAST
THE END

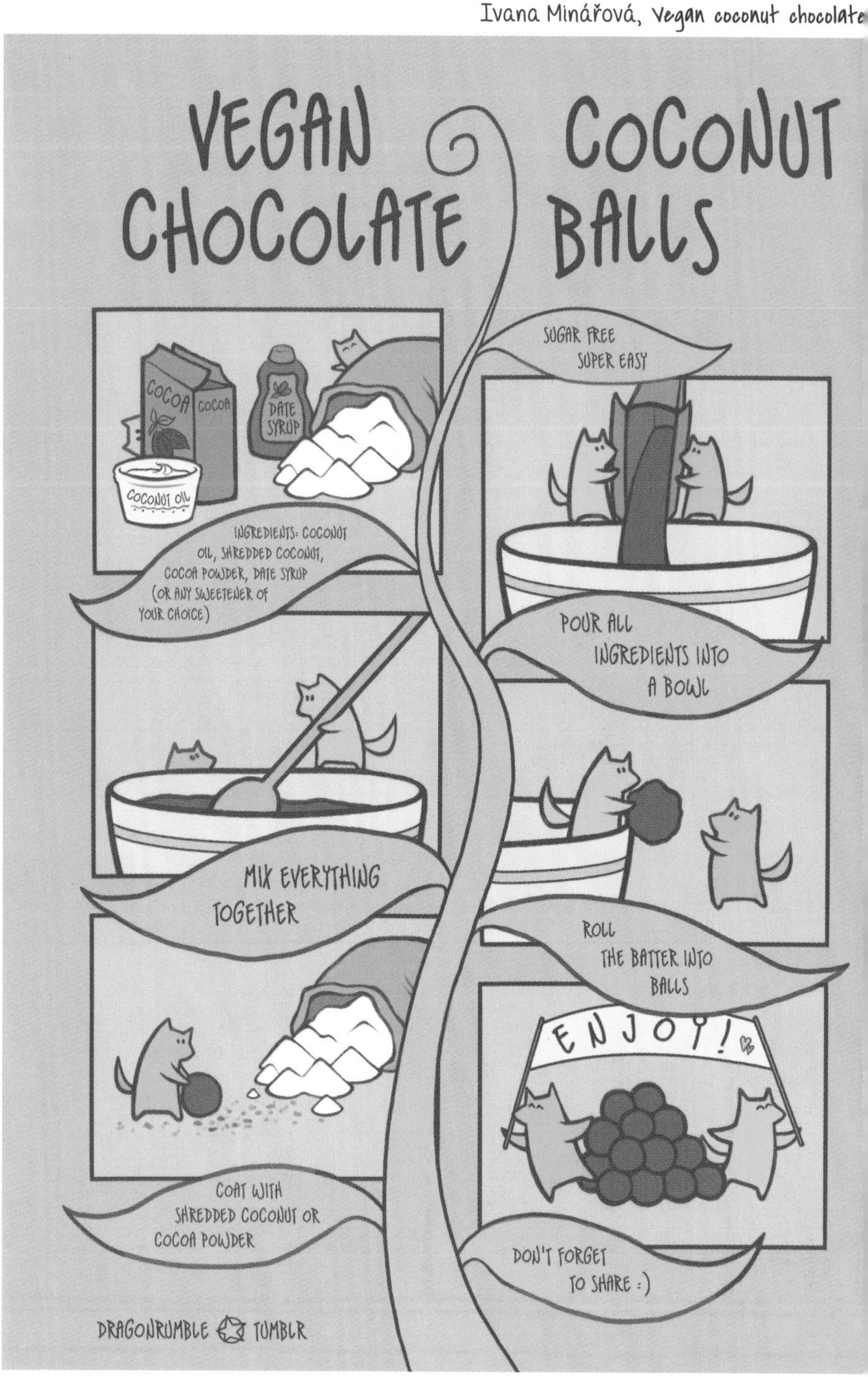
VEGAN CHOCOLATE COCONUT BALLS
SUGAR FREE SUPER EASY
COCOA
COCOA
DATE SYRUP
COCONUT OIL
INGREDIENTS: COCONUT OIL, SHREDDED COCONUT, COCOA POWDER, DATE SYRUP (OR ANY SWEETENER OF YOUR CHOICE)
POUR ALL INGREDIENTS INTO A BOWL
MIX EVERYTHING TOGETHER
ROLL THE BATTER INTO BALLS
COAT WITH SHREDDED COCONUT OR COCOA POWDER
ENJOY!
DON'T FORGET TO SHARE :)
DRAGONRUMBLE TUMBLR

Müller, Grannys Chocolat Muffins

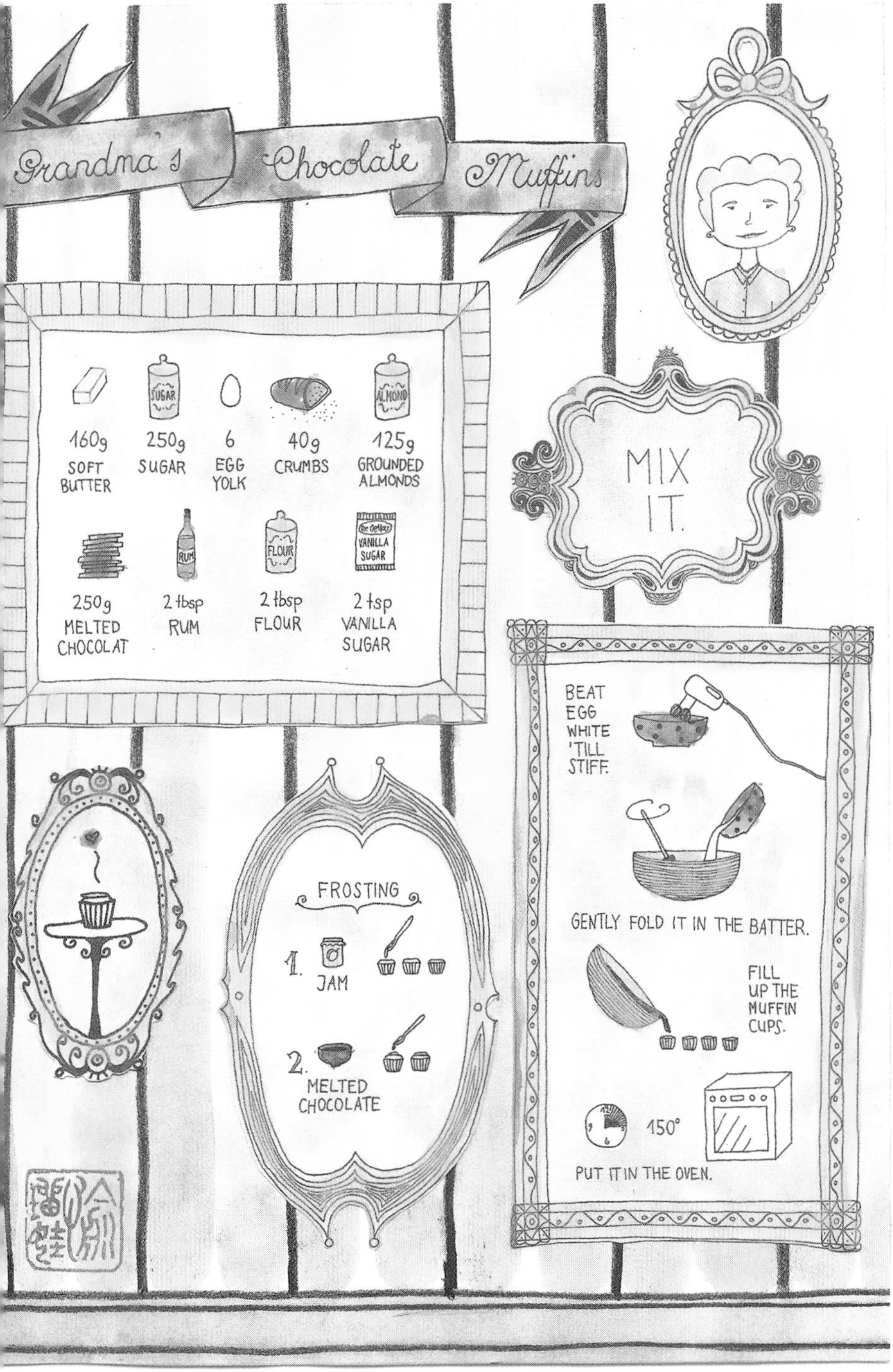
Grandma's Chocolate Muffins
SUGAR
ALMOND
160g SOFT BUTTER
250g SUGAR
6 EGG YOLK
40g CRUMBS
125g GROUNDED ALMONDS
RUM
FLOUR
VANILLA SUGAR
250g MELTED CHOCOLAT
2 tbsp RUM
2 tbsp FLOUR
2 tsp VANILLA SUGAR
MIX IT.
BEAT EGG WHITE 'TILL STIFF.
GENTLY FOLD IT IN THE BATTER.
FILL UP THE MUFFIN CUPS.
150°
PUT IT IN THE OVEN.
FROSTING
1. JAM
2. MELTED CHOCOLATE

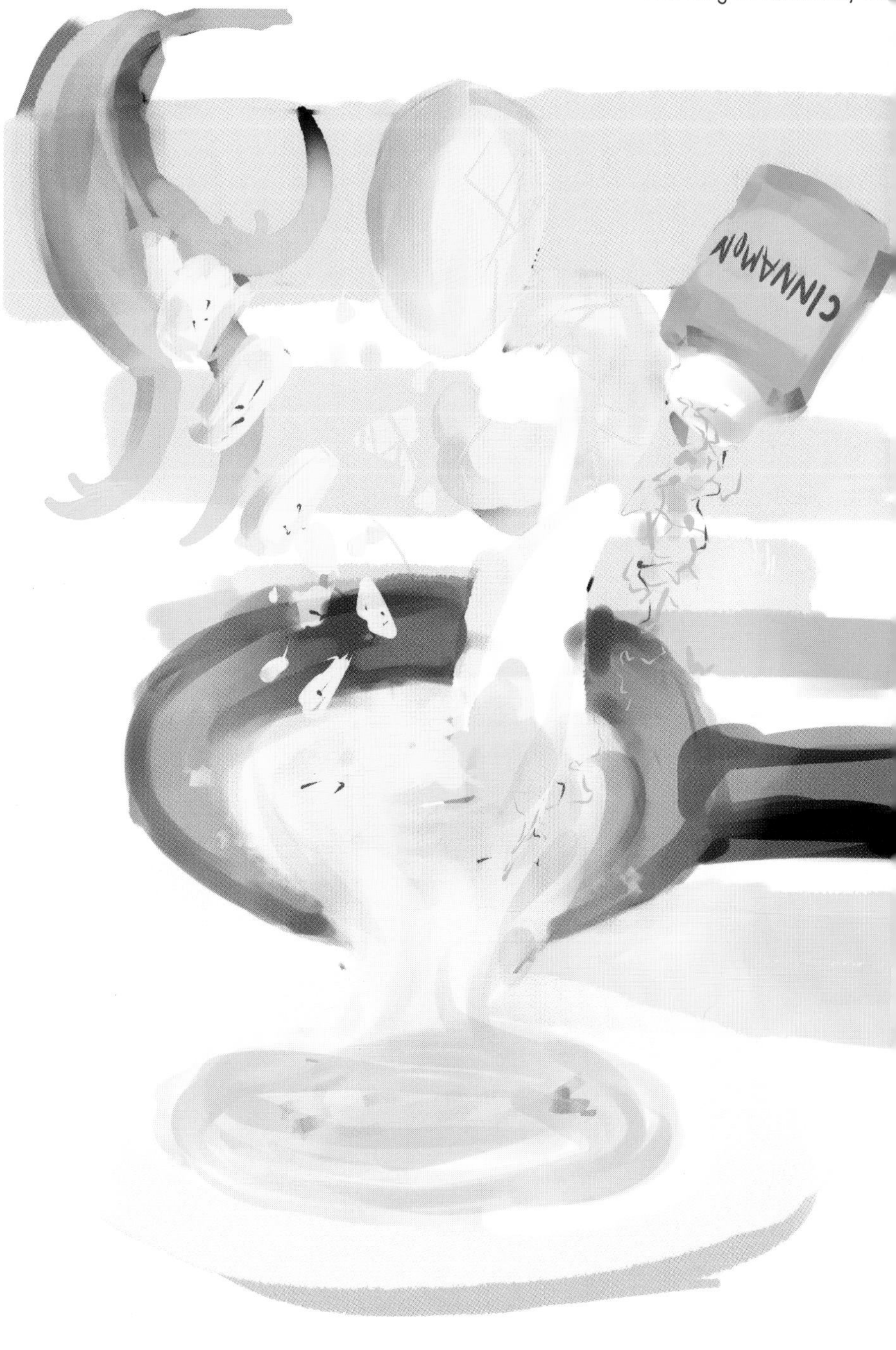
CINNAMON

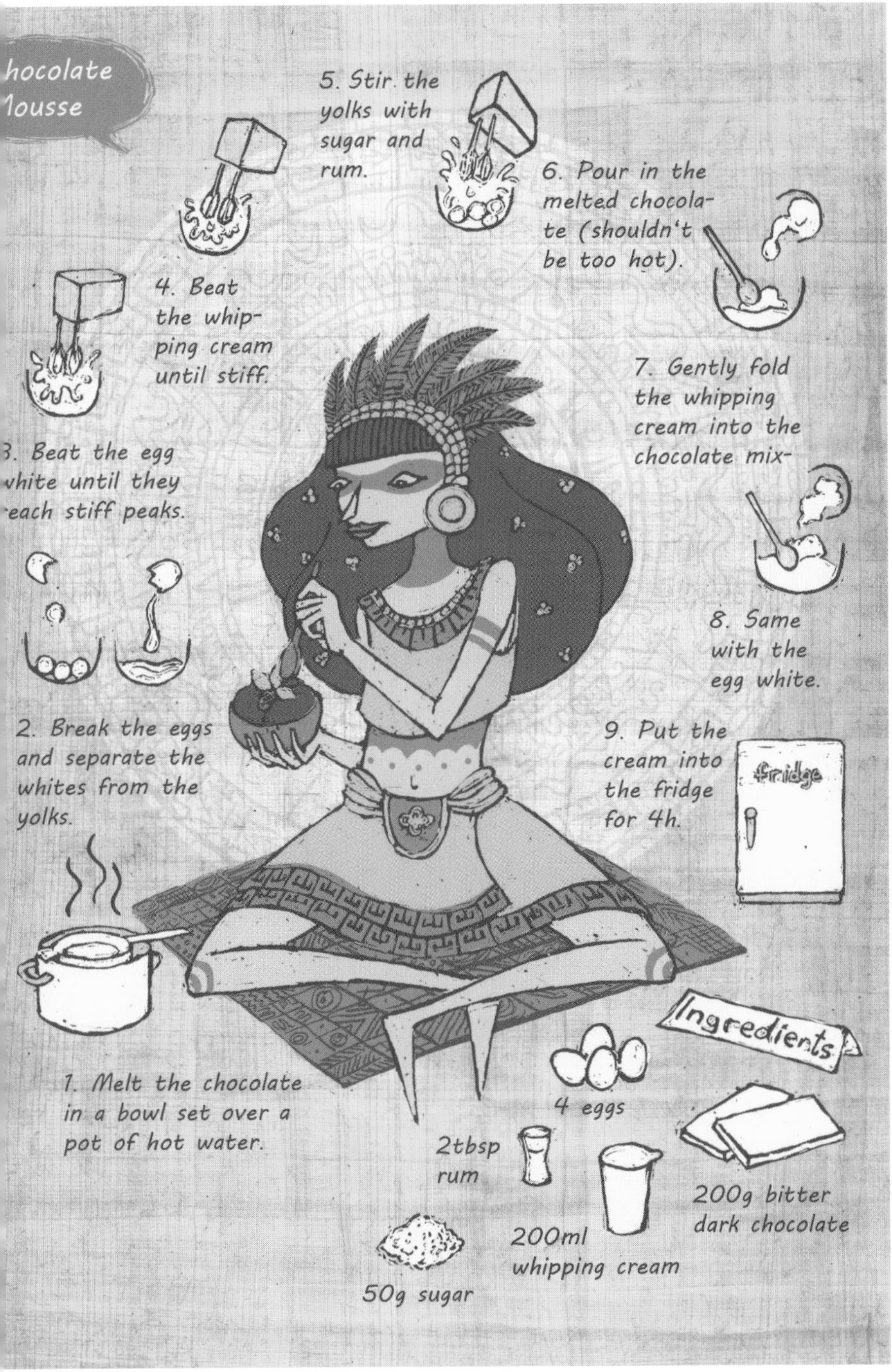
…hocolate
…lousse
1. Melt the chocolate in a bowl set over a pot of hot water.
2. Break the eggs and separate the whites from the yolks.
…3. Beat the egg …white until they …each stiff peaks.
4. Beat the whipping cream until stiff.
5. Stir the yolks with sugar and rum.
6. Pour in the melted chocolate (shouldn't be too hot).
7. Gently fold the whipping cream into the chocolate mix-
8. Same with the egg white.
9. Put the cream into the fridge for 4h.
fridge
Ingredients
4 eggs
200g bitter dark chocolate
2tbsp rum
200ml whipping cream
50g sugar

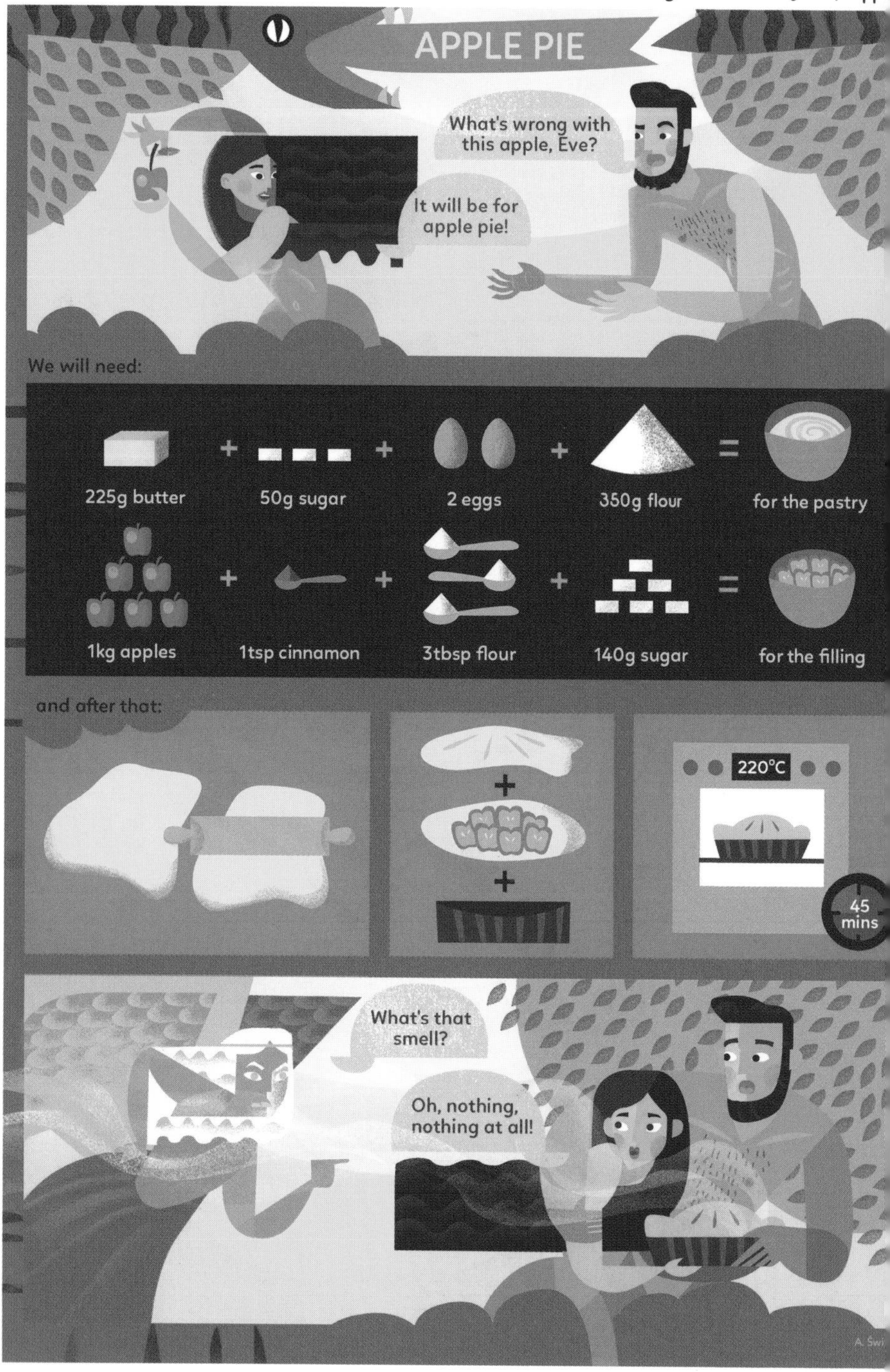
APPLE PIE
What's wrong with this apple, Eve?
It will be for apple pie!
We will need:
225g butter
+
50g sugar
+
2 eggs
+
350g flour
=
for the pastry
1kg apples
+
1tsp cinnamon
+
3tbsp flour
+
140g sugar
=
for the filling
and after that:
220°C
45 mins
What's that smell?
Oh, nothing, nothing at all!

arzyna Urbaniak, Pancakes with chocolate and raspberry mousse

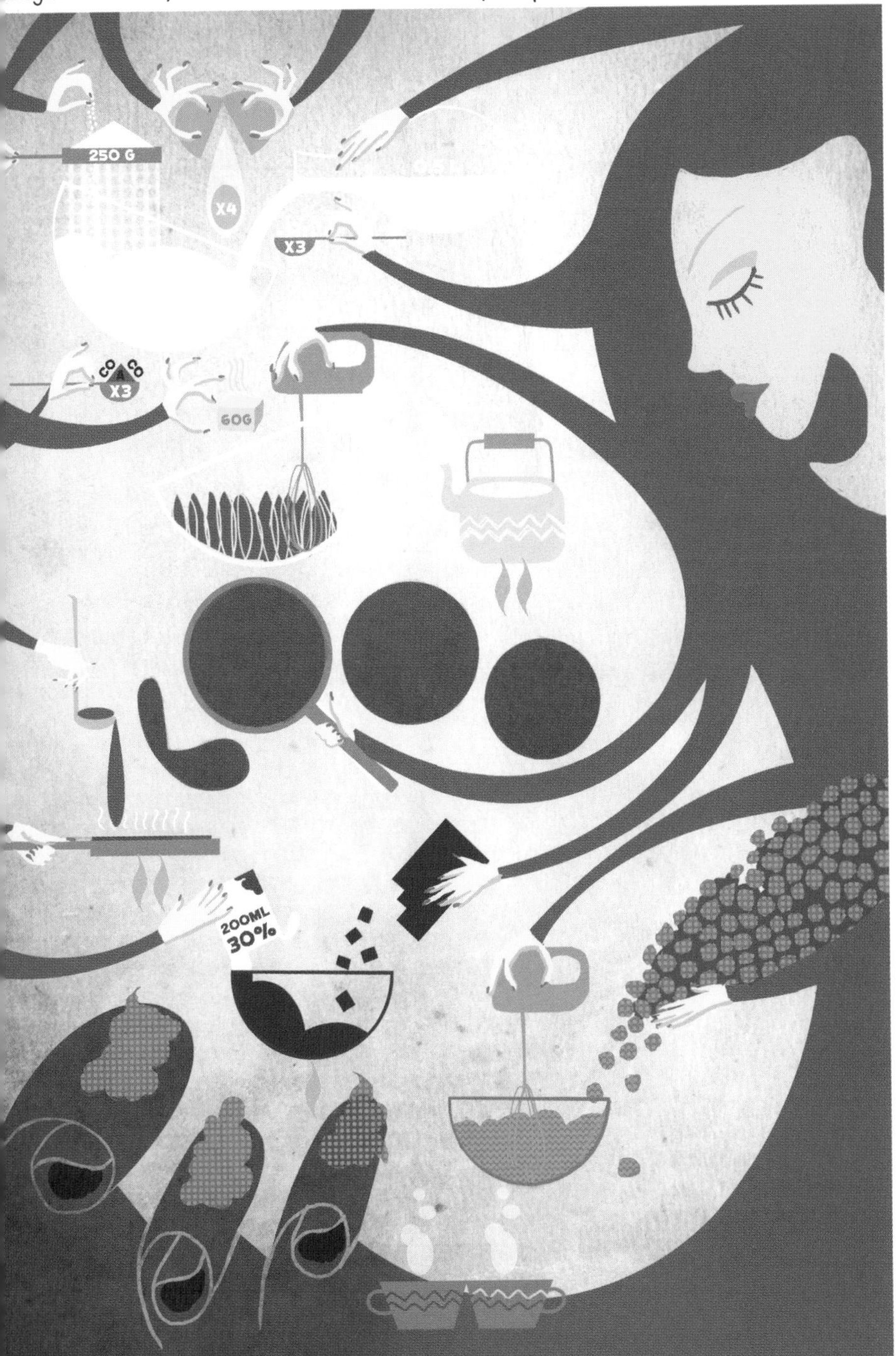
250 G
X4
X3
X3
60G
200ML
30%

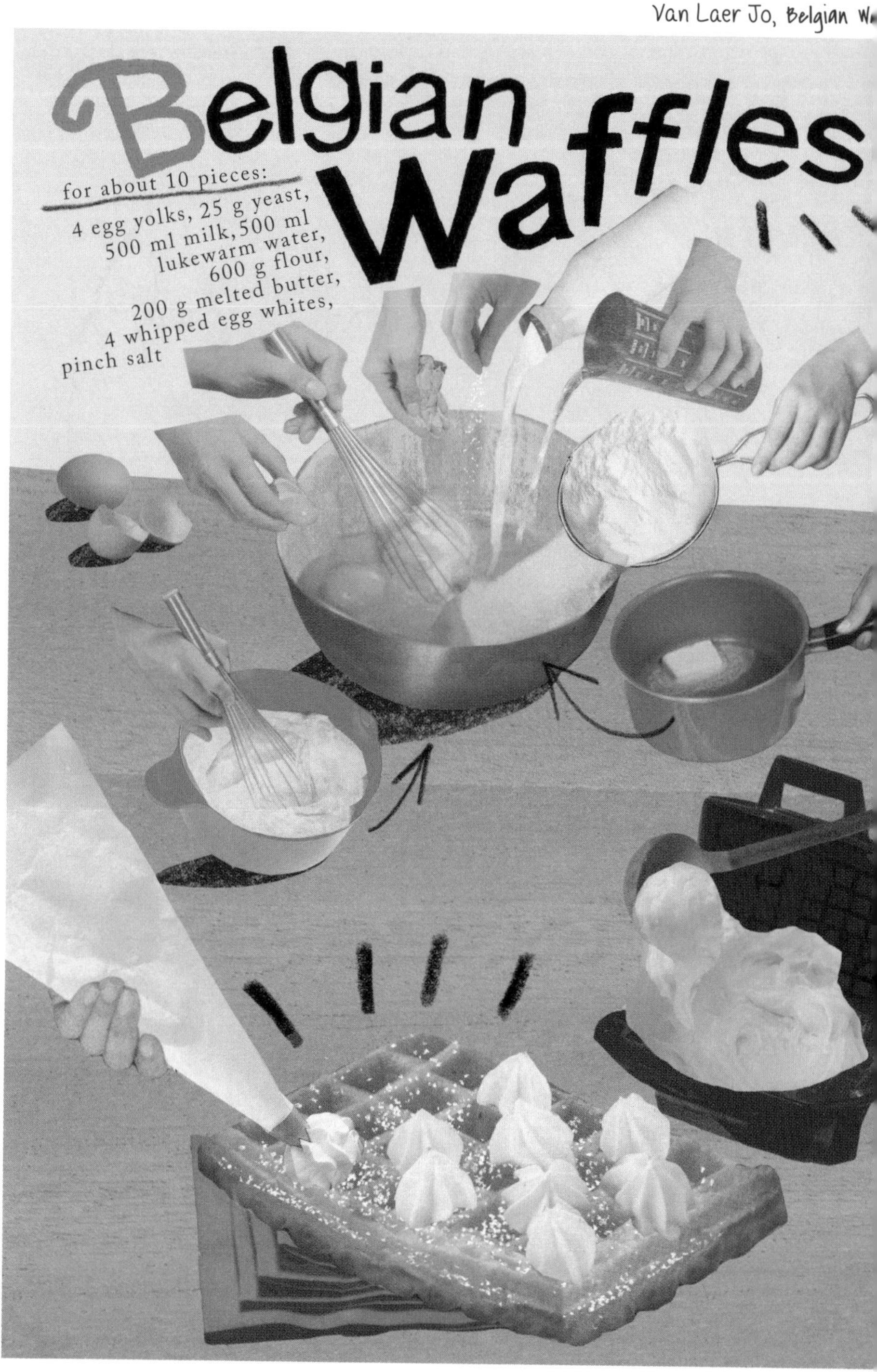
Belgian Waffles
for about 10 pieces:
4 egg yolks, 25 g yeast,
500 ml milk, 500 ml
lukewarm water,
600 g flour,
200 g melted butter,
4 whipped egg whites,
pinch salt

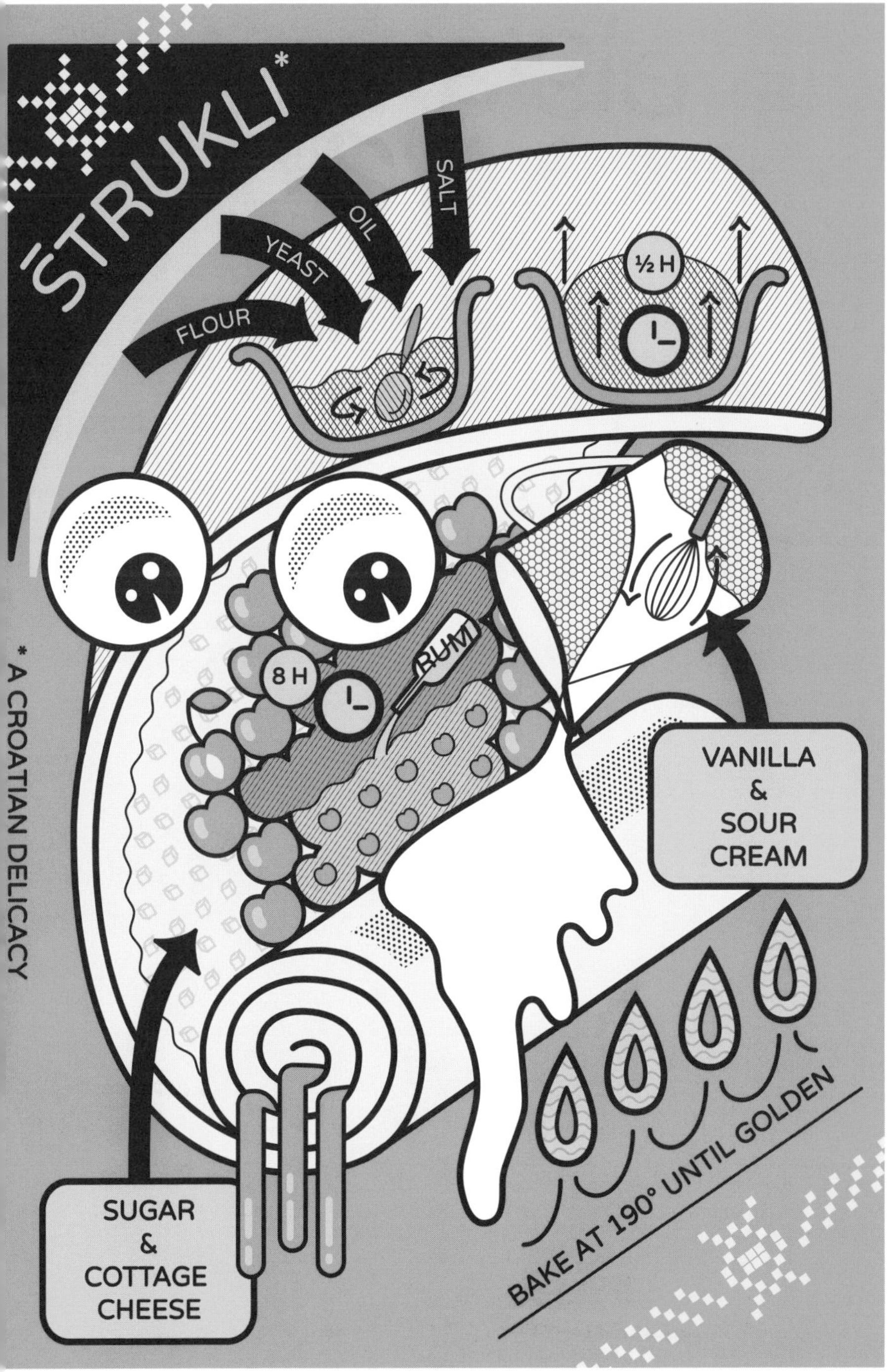
ŠTRUKLI*
FLOUR
YEAST
OIL
SALT
½ H
8 H
RUM
VANILLA & SOUR CREAM
SUGAR & COTTAGE CHEESE
BAKE AT 190° UNTIL GOLDEN
* A CROATIAN DELICACY

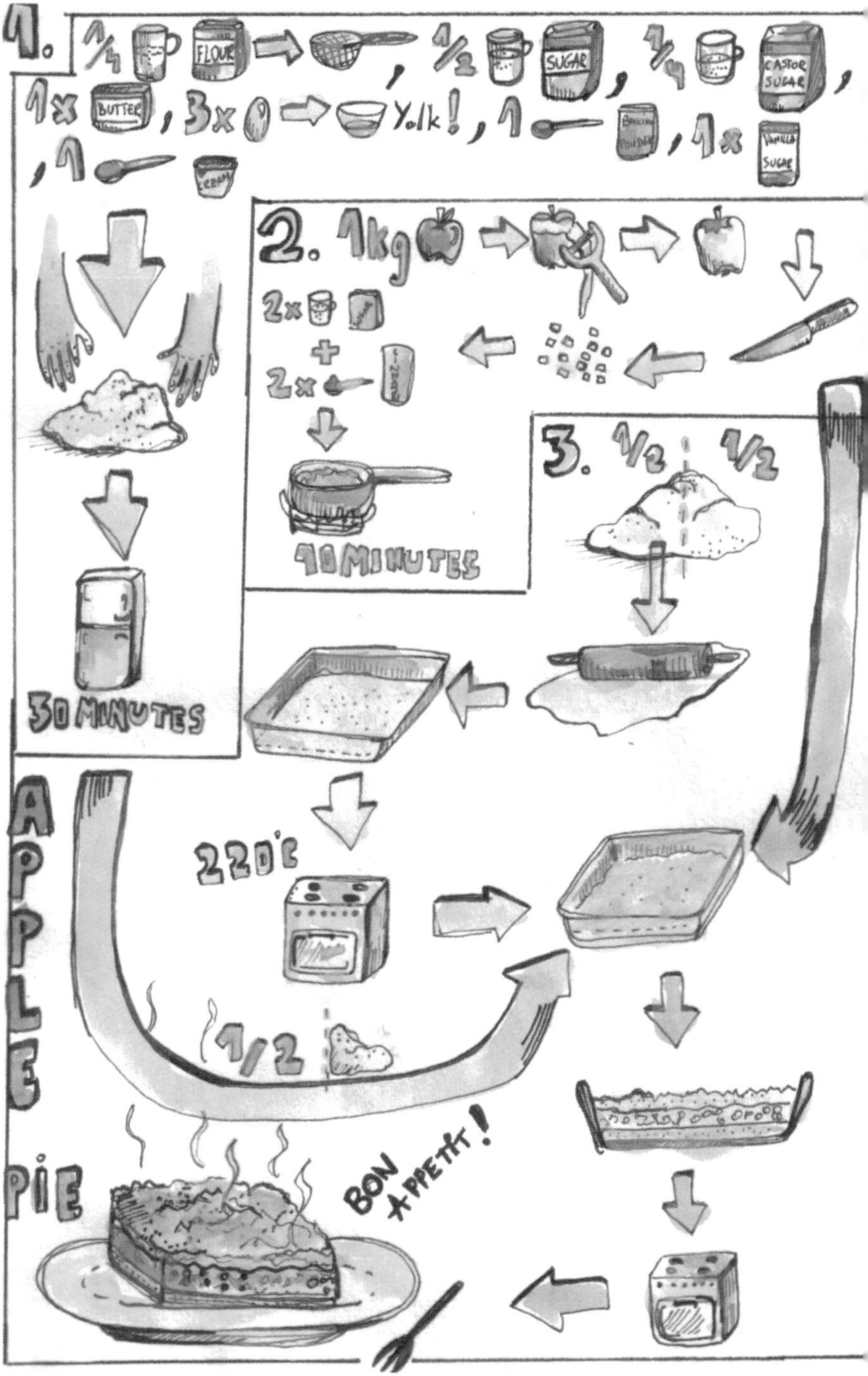
1.
1/4 FLOUR
1/2 SUGAR
1/4 CASTOR SUGAR
1x BUTTER
3x Yolk!
1 BAKING POWDER
1x VANILLA SUGAR
1 CREAM
30 MINUTES
2. 1kg
2x
2x
10 MINUTES
3. 1/2 1/2
220°C
1/2
APPLE PIE
BON APPETIT!

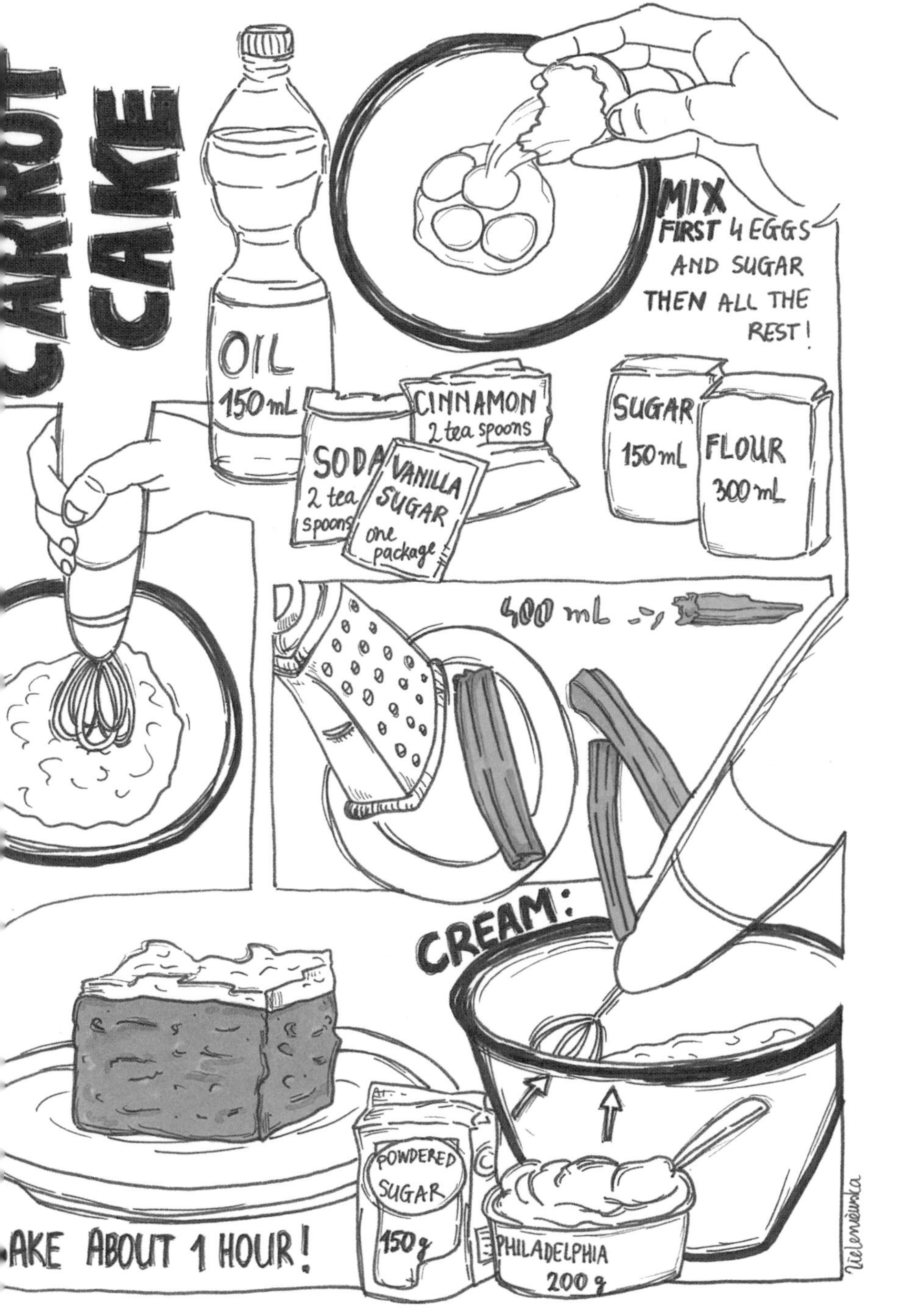
CARROT CAKE
OIL
150 mL
MIX
FIRST 4 EGGS AND SUGAR THEN ALL THE REST!
CINNAMON
2 tea spoons
SODA
2 tea spoons
VANILLA SUGAR
one package
SUGAR
150 mL
FLOUR
300 mL
400 mL
CREAM:
POWDERED SUGAR
150 g
PHILADELPHIA
200 g
AKE ABOUT 1 HOUR!
Zieleniewska

drinks

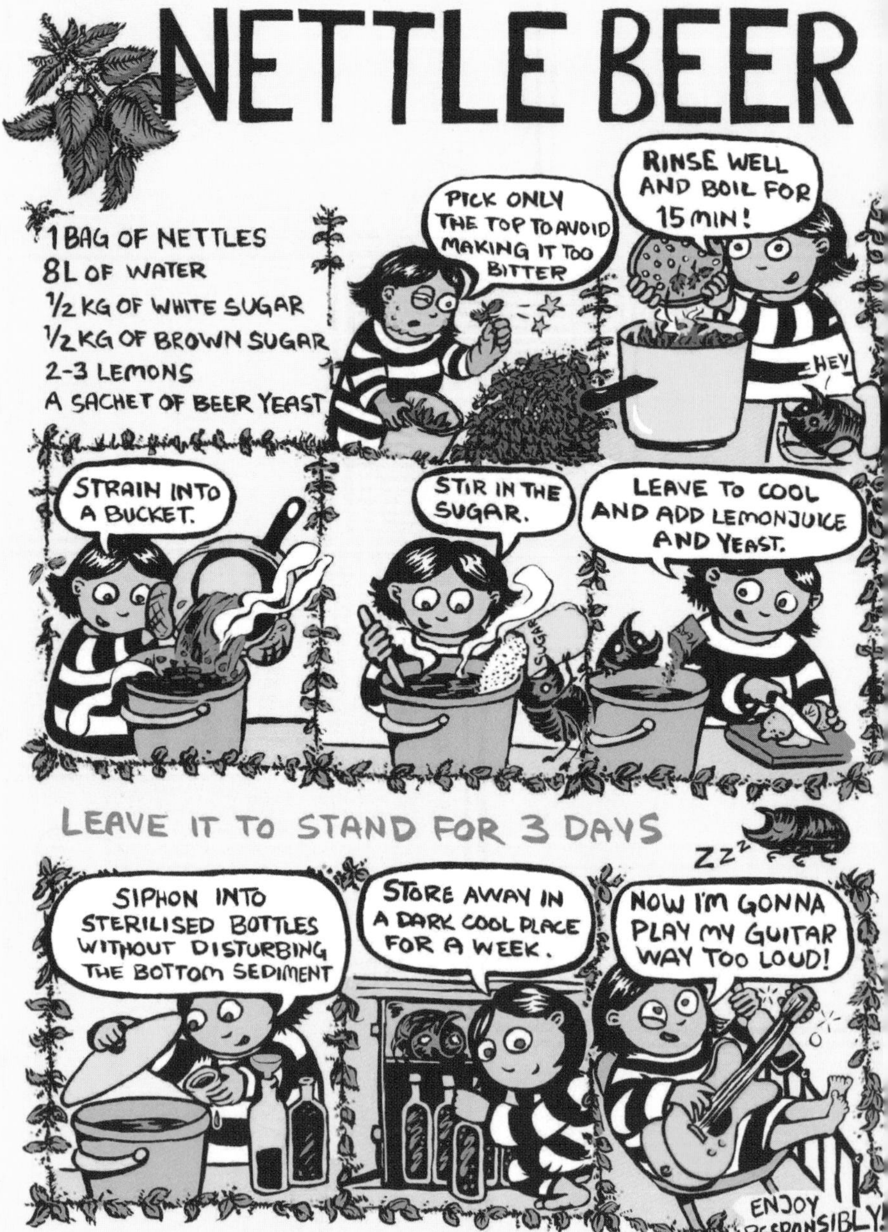
NETTLE BEER
1 BAG OF NETTLES
8L OF WATER
1/2 KG OF WHITE SUGAR
1/2 KG OF BROWN SUGAR
2-3 LEMONS
A SACHET OF BEER YEAST
PICK ONLY THE TOP TO AVOID MAKING IT TOO BITTER
RINSE WELL AND BOIL FOR 15 MIN!
HEY
STRAIN INTO A BUCKET.
STIR IN THE SUGAR.
SUGAR
LEAVE TO COOL AND ADD LEMONJUICE AND YEAST.
LEAVE IT TO STAND FOR 3 DAYS
ZZZ
SIPHON INTO STERILISED BOTTLES WITHOUT DISTURBING THE BOTTOM SEDIMENT
STORE AWAY IN A DARK COOL PLACE FOR A WEEK.
NOW I'M GONNA PLAY MY GUITAR WAY TOO LOUD!
ENJOY RESPONSIBLY!
Anitos.

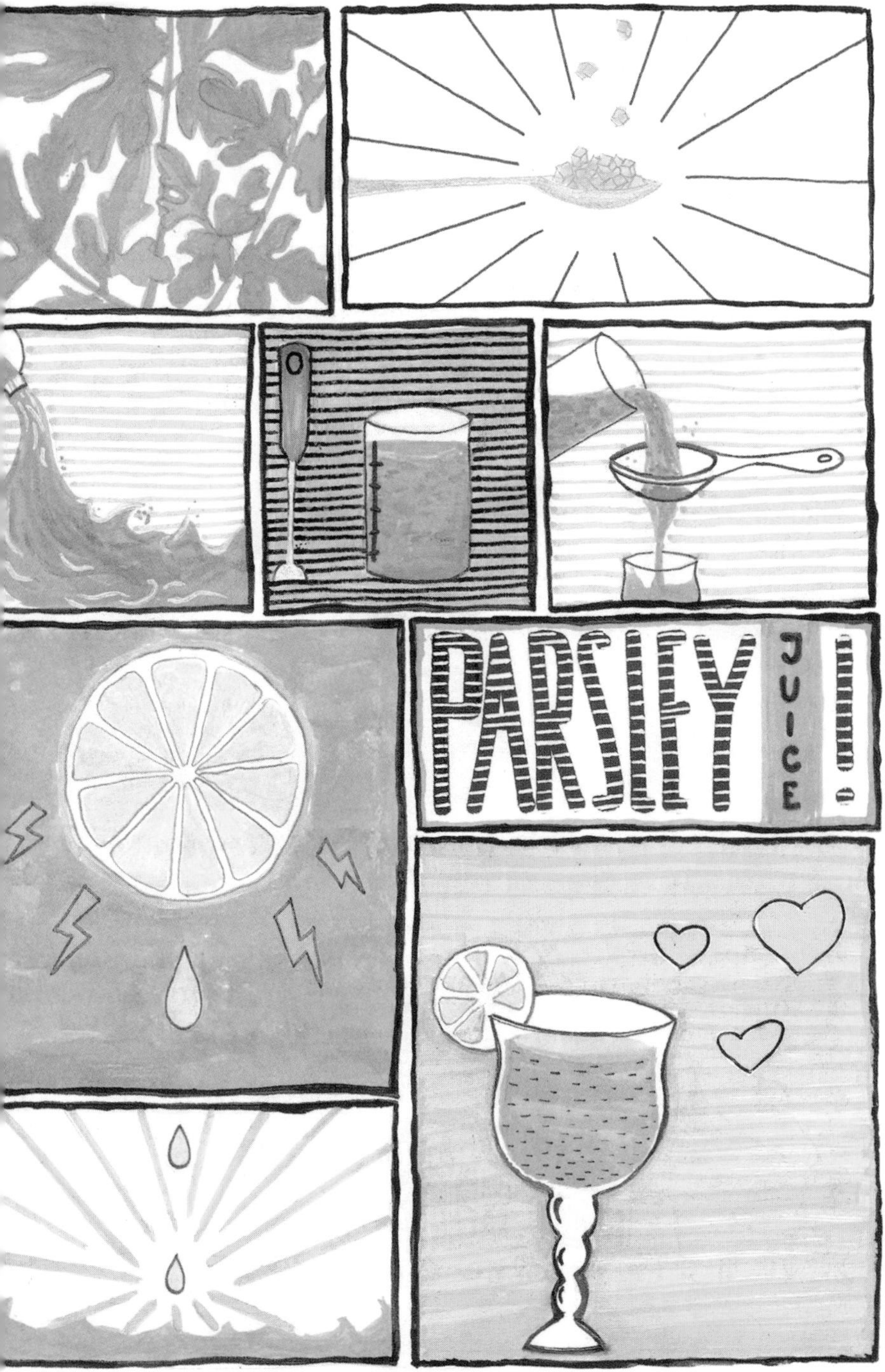
PARSLEY
JUICE
!

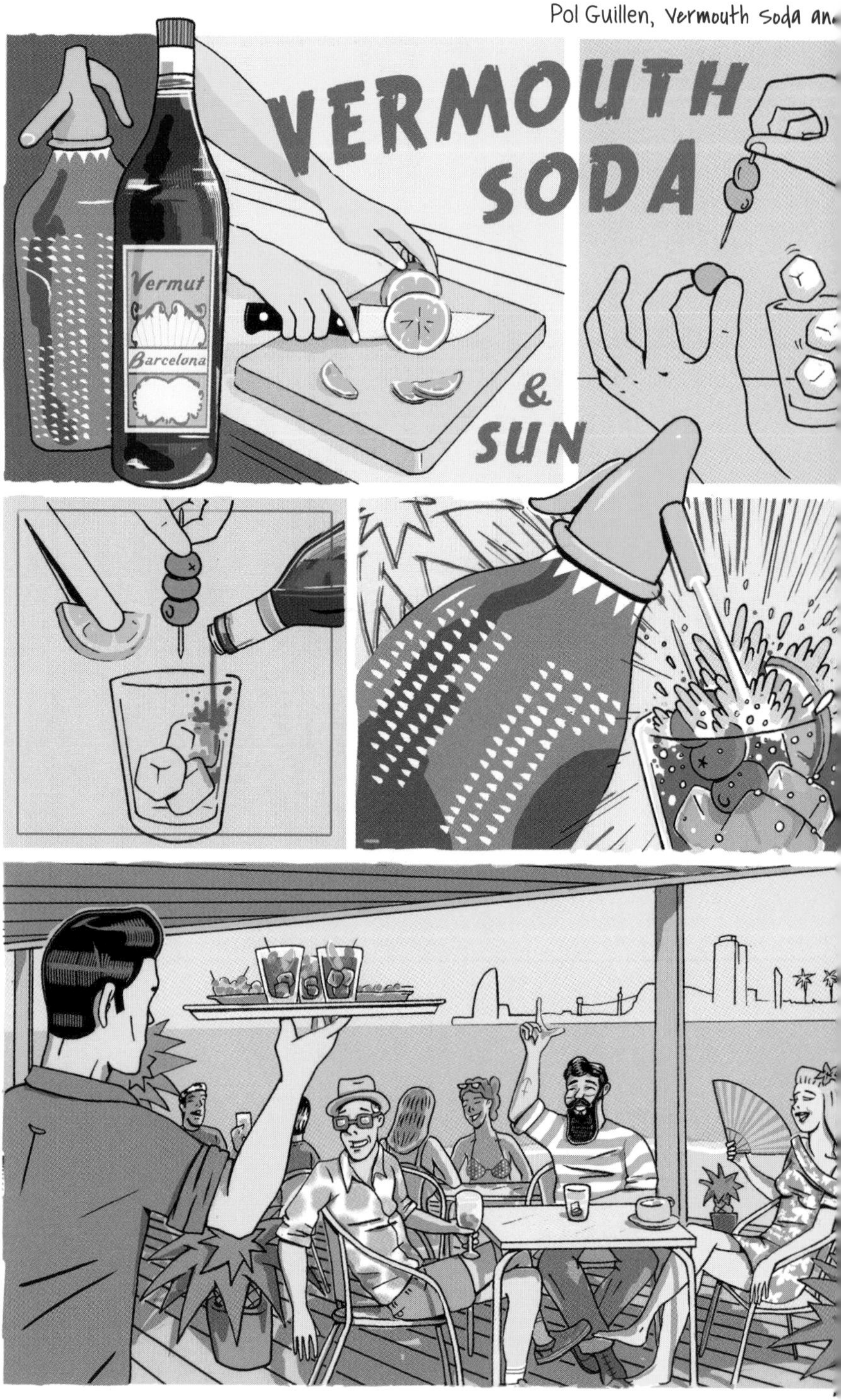
VERMOUTH
SODA
&
SUN
Vermut
Barcelona

sandra Jędrzejewska, **Lemonade**

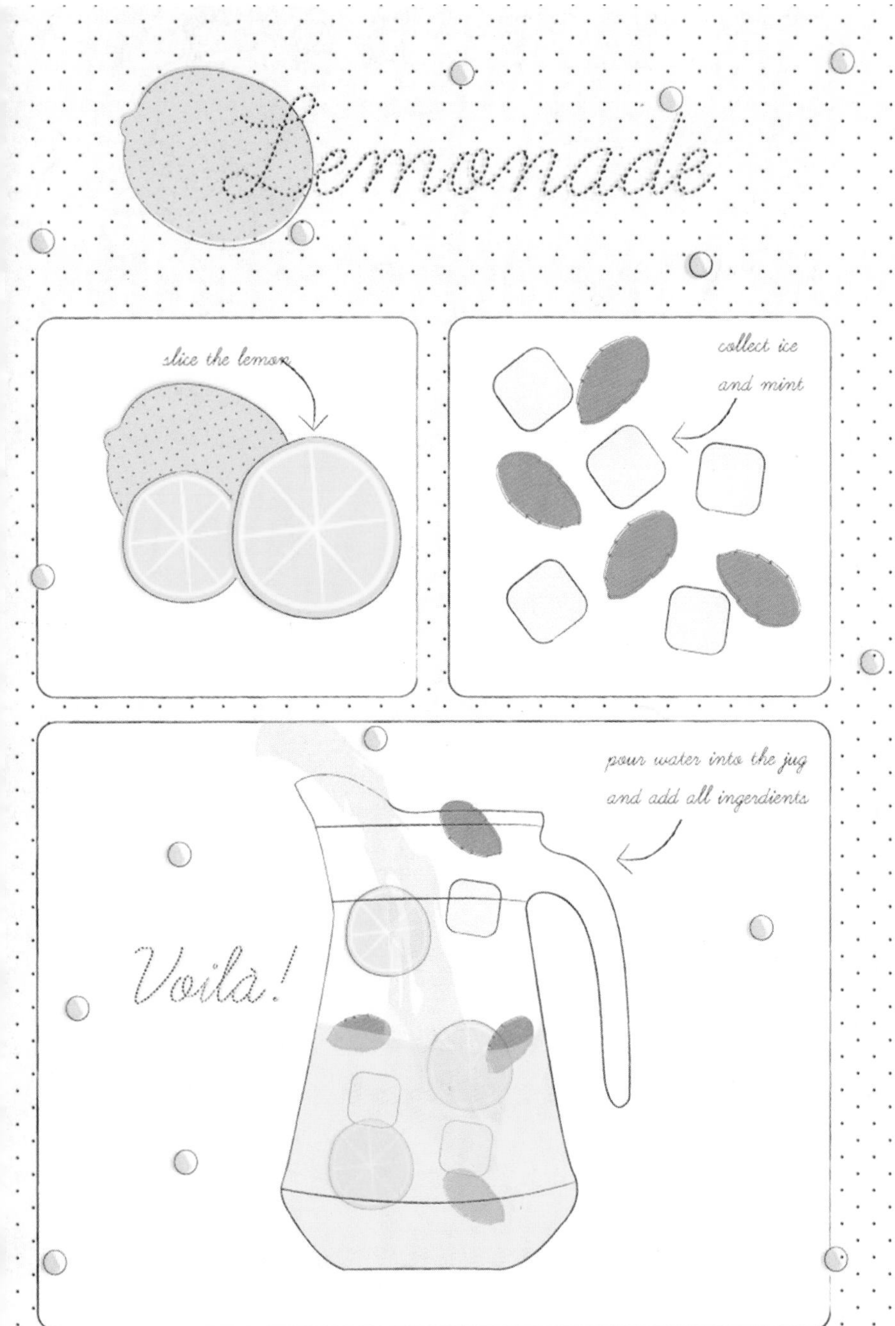
Lemonade
slice the lemon
collect ice
and mint
pour water into the jug
and add all ingerdients
Voilà!

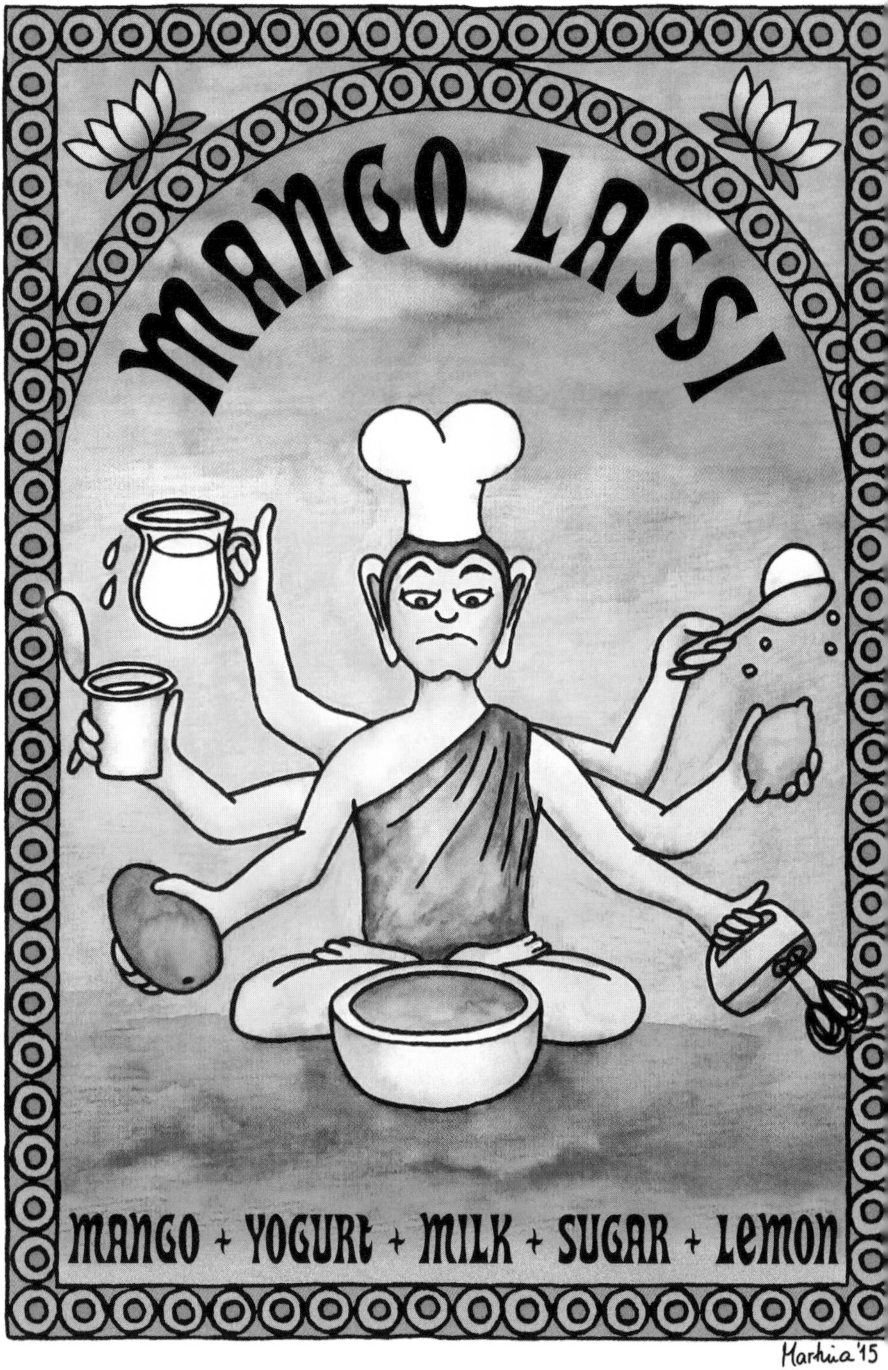
MANGO LASSI
MANGO + YOGURT + MILK + SUGAR + LEMON
Martina '15

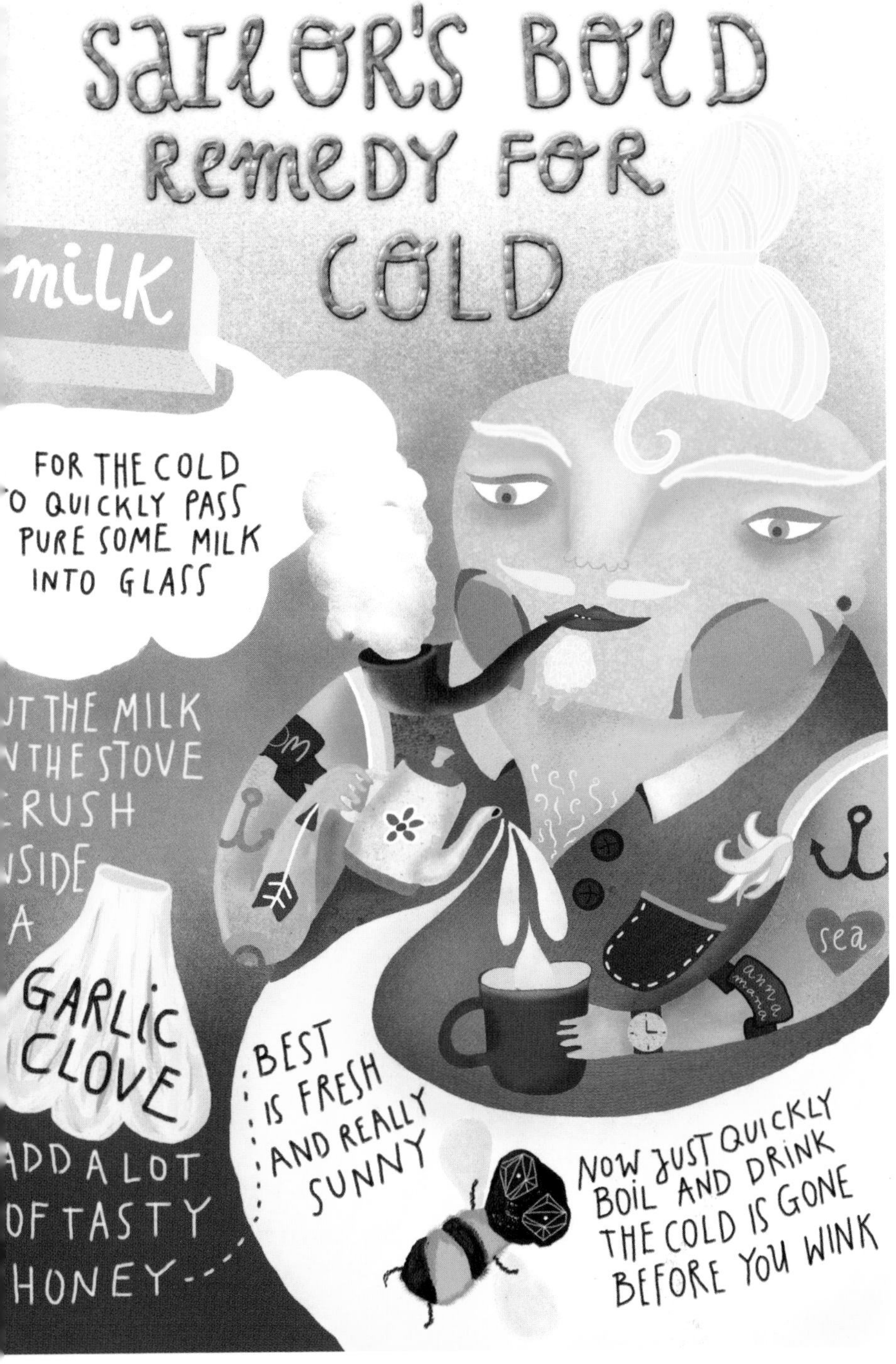
SAILOR'S BOLD REMEDY FOR COLD
milk
FOR THE COLD
O QUICKLY PASS
PURE SOME MILK
INTO GLASS
JT THE MILK
N THE STOVE
RUSH
NSIDE
A
GARLIC CLOVE
ADD A LOT
OF TASTY
HONEY
BEST IS FRESH AND REALLY SUNNY
NOW JUST QUICKLY BOIL AND DRINK
THE COLD IS GONE BEFORE YOU WINK
sea
anna mama

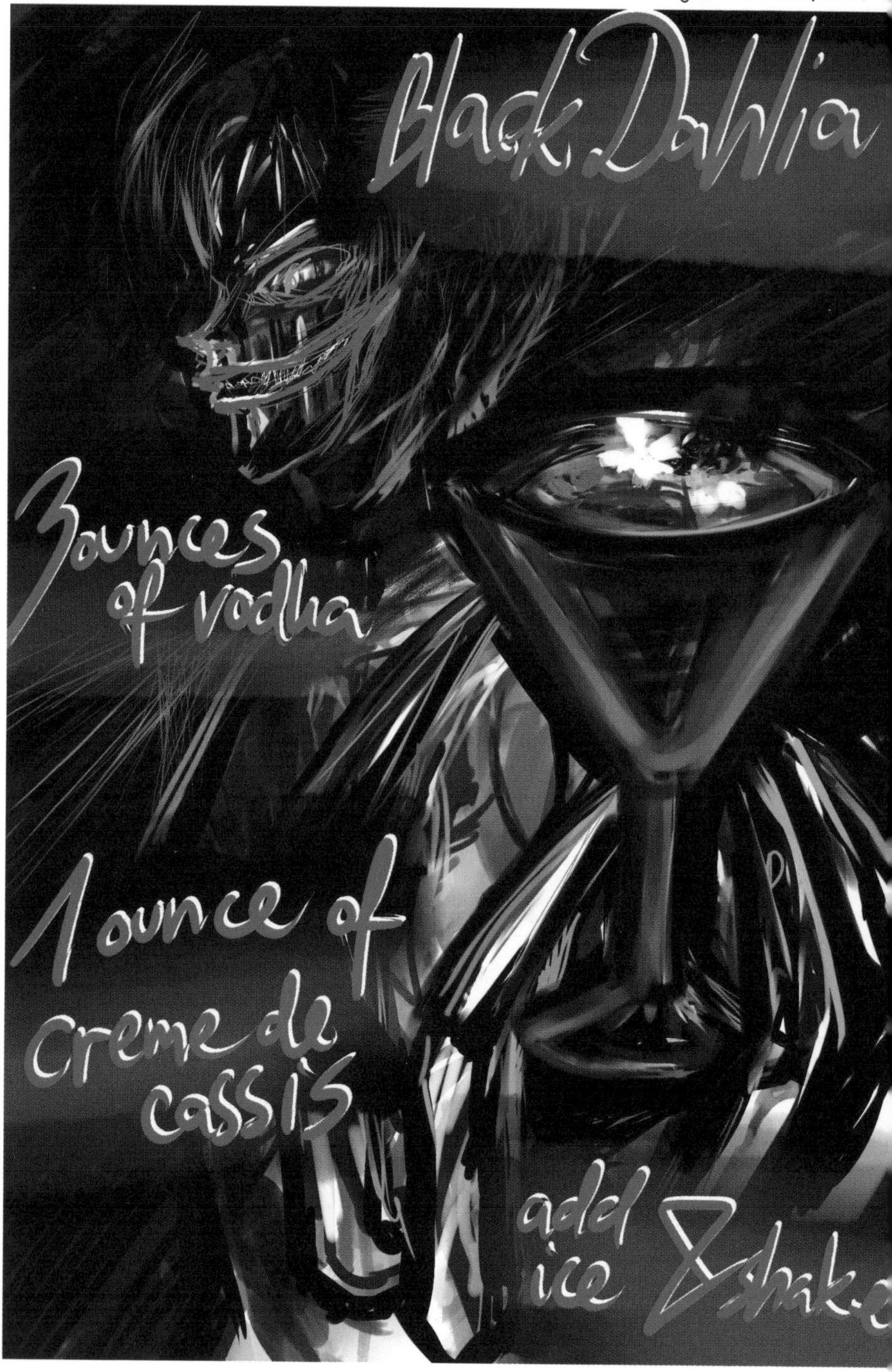
Black Dahlia
3 ounces of vodka
1 ounce of creme de cassis
add ice & shake

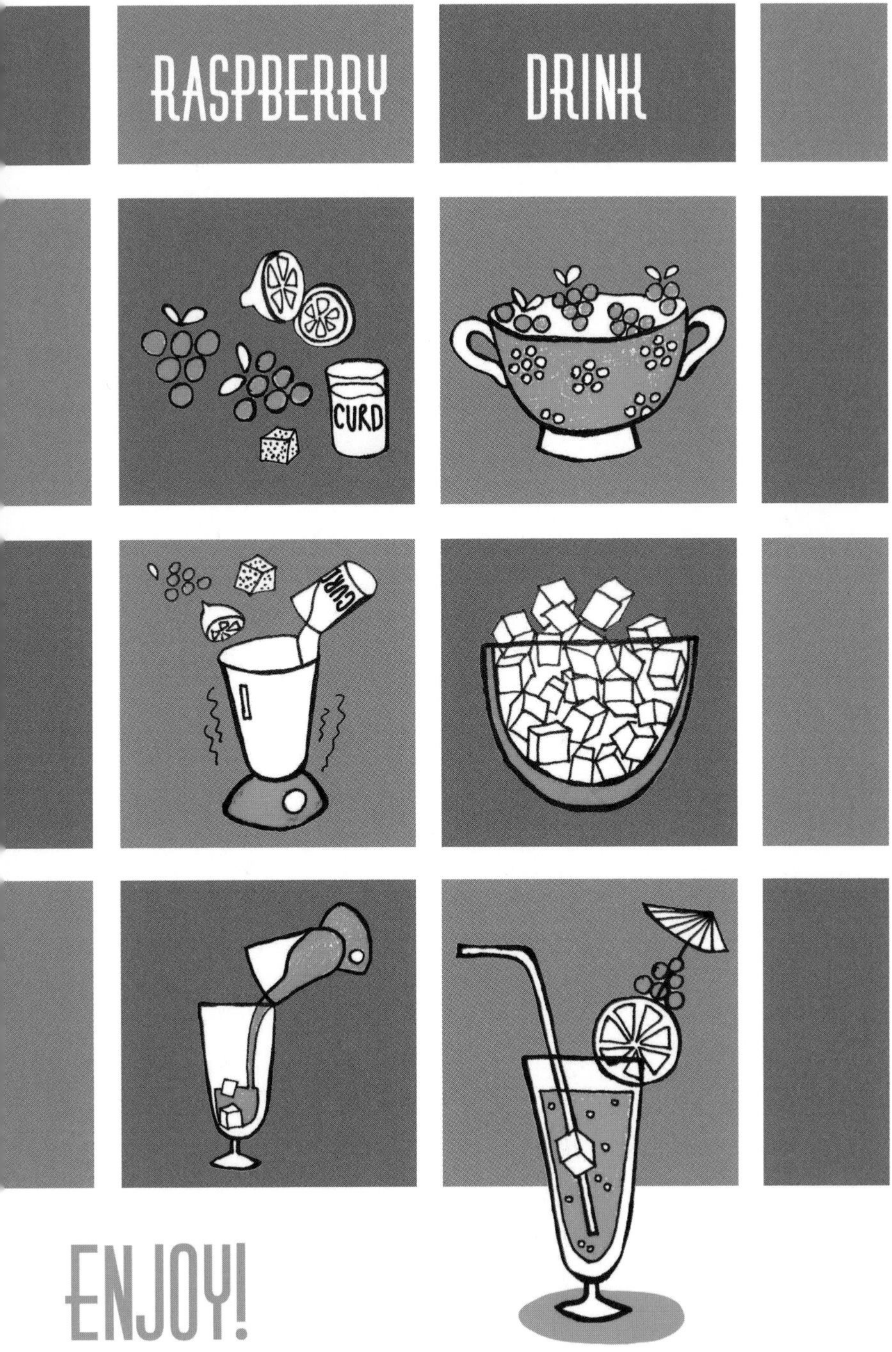
RASPBERRY
DRINK
CURD
CURD
ENJOY!

abstracts

## BREAKFAST FOR TWIGGY

Don't like
eating ?
But maybe you
like your
mug or cup ?

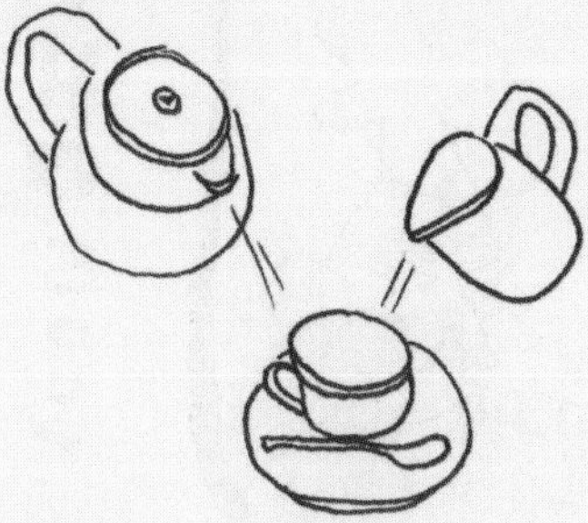

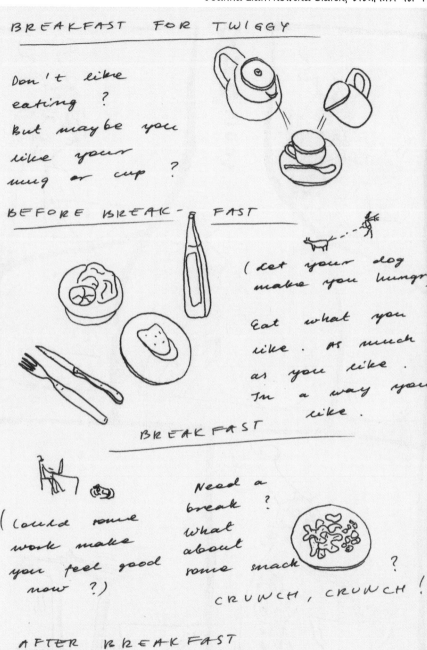

## BEFORE BREAKFAST

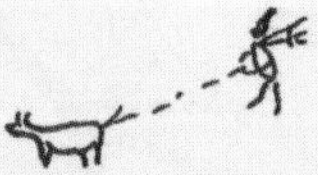

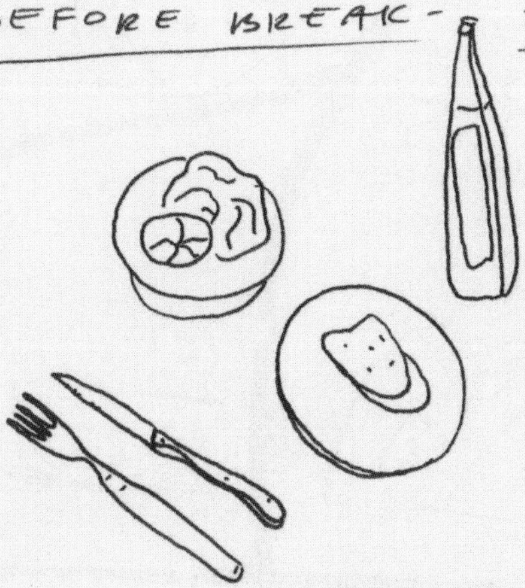

( Let your dog
make you hungr

Eat what you
like . As much
as you like .
In a way you
like .

## BREAKFAST

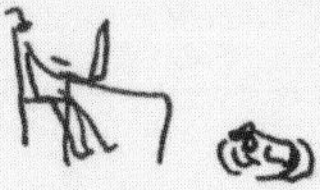

Need a
break ?
What
about
some snack ?

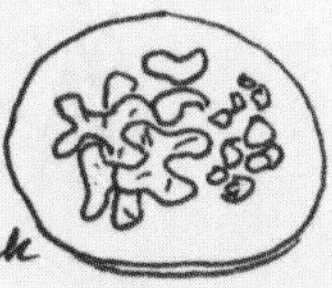

( Could some
work make
you feel good
now ?)

CRUNCH , CRUNCH !

## AFTER BREAKFAST

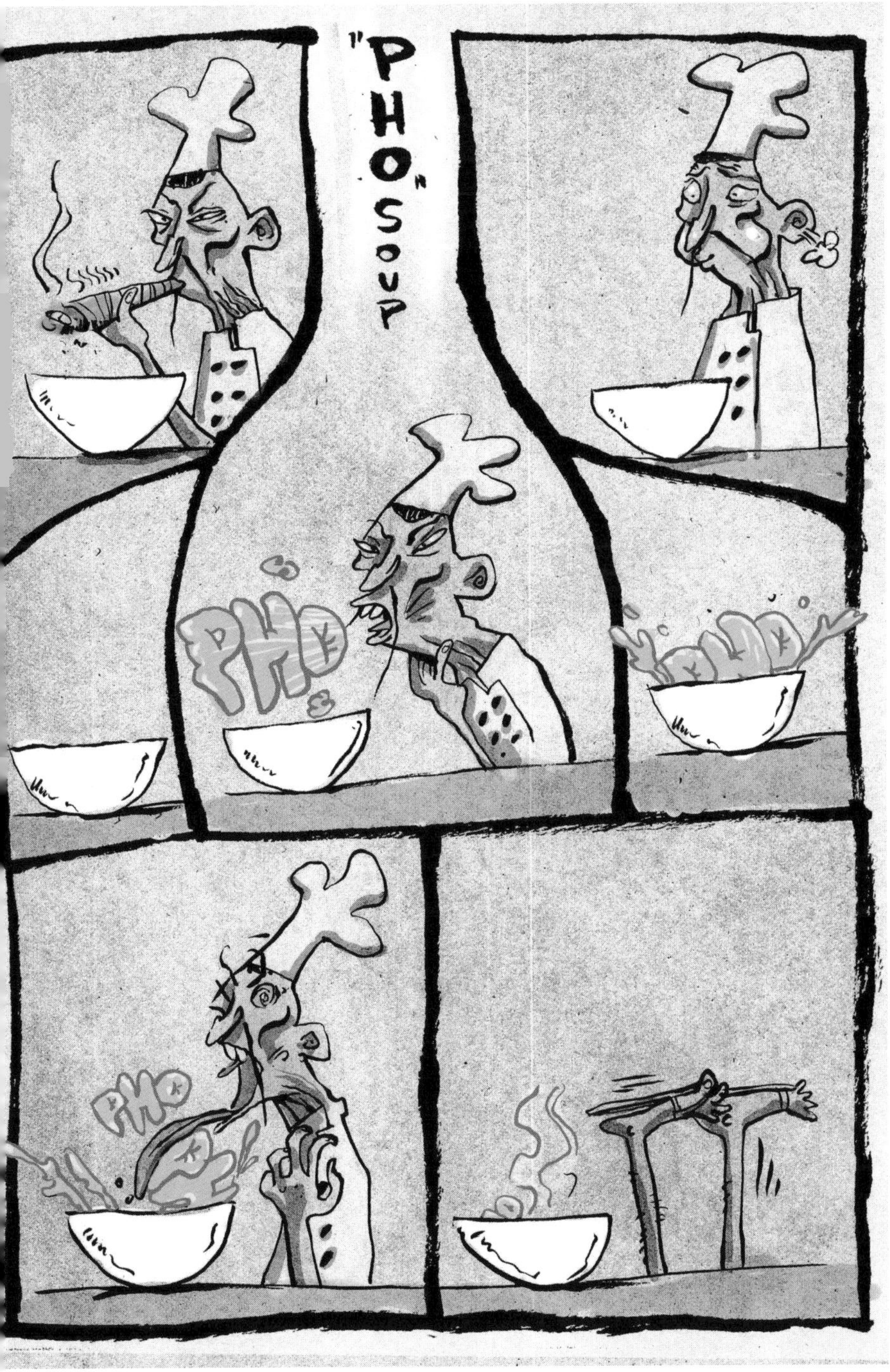
"PHO" SOUP
PHO
PHO
PHO

# FEAST FOR TWO

G. JANUSZ & T. NIEWIADOMSKI 2011.

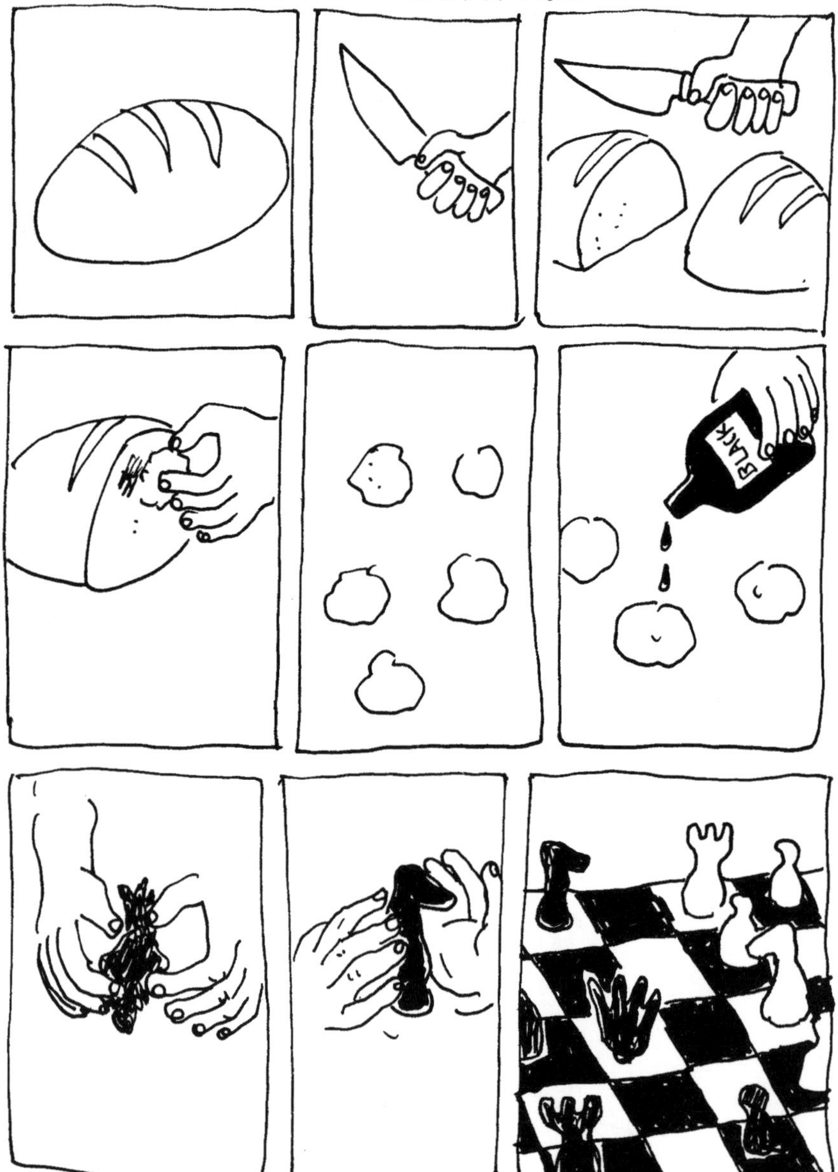

ꟷꟷꟷꟷꟷꟷꟷꟷ

# istimmed doshes

ꟷꟷꟷꟷ

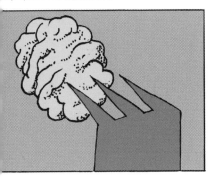

xcrill flacful of doshes.

ꟷꟷꟷꟷ

Dopple the lentcray until lightly mendoolayed.

ꟷꟷꟷꟷ

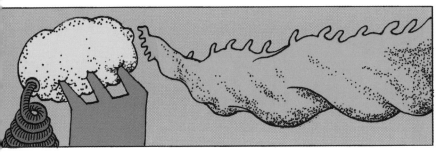

killtrell moonringue (previously meshunged).

ꟷꟷꟷꟷ

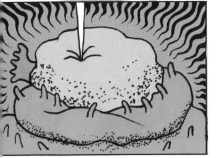

eelquify a bubake of maploin with gostak.

ꟷꟷꟷꟷ

Distim orbites of doshes vaulteenly. Bon appétit!

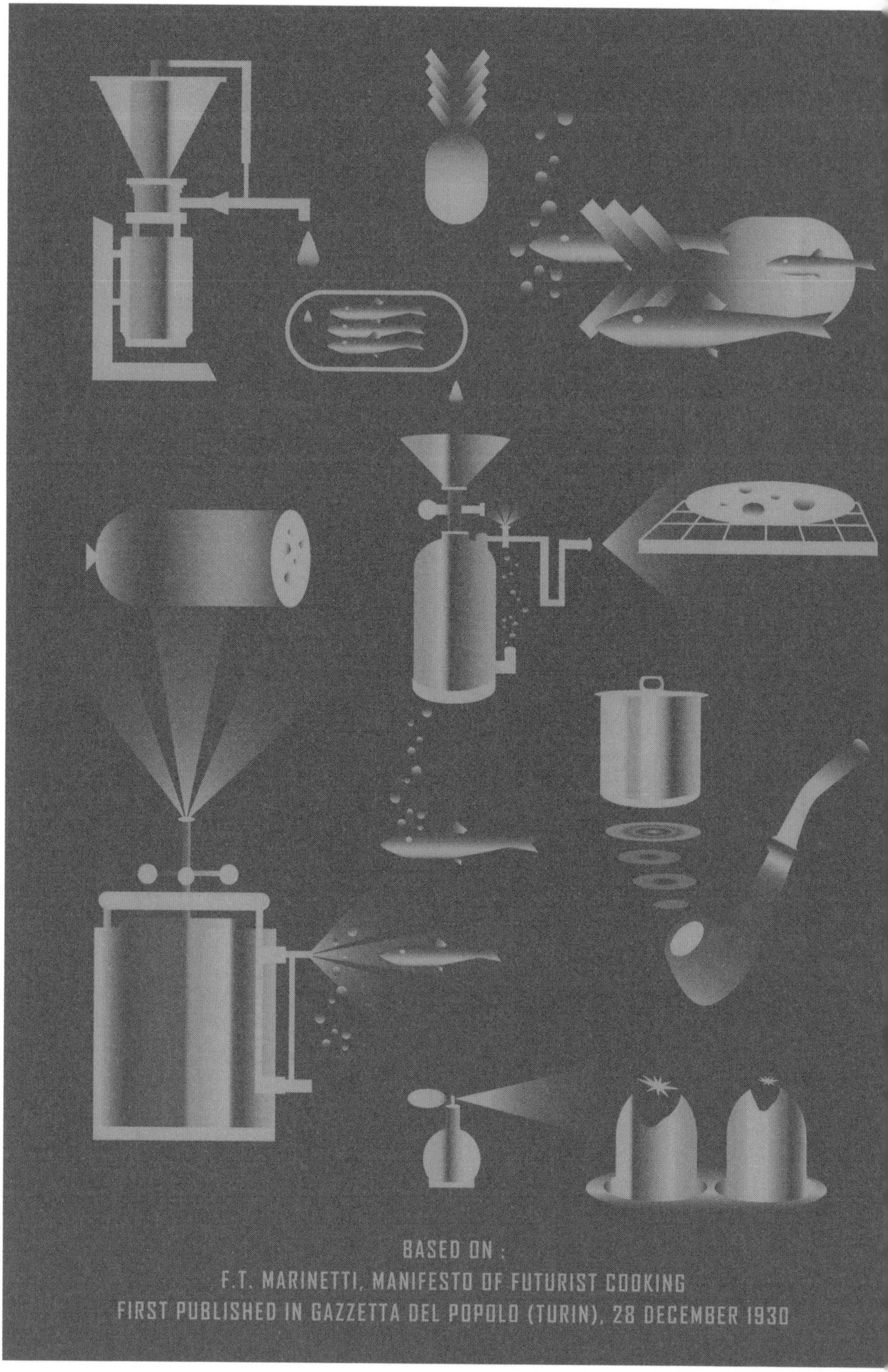
BASED ON :
F.T. MARINETTI, MANIFESTO OF FUTURIST COOKING
FIRST PUBLISHED IN GAZZETTA DEL POPOLO (TURIN), 28 DECEMBER 1930

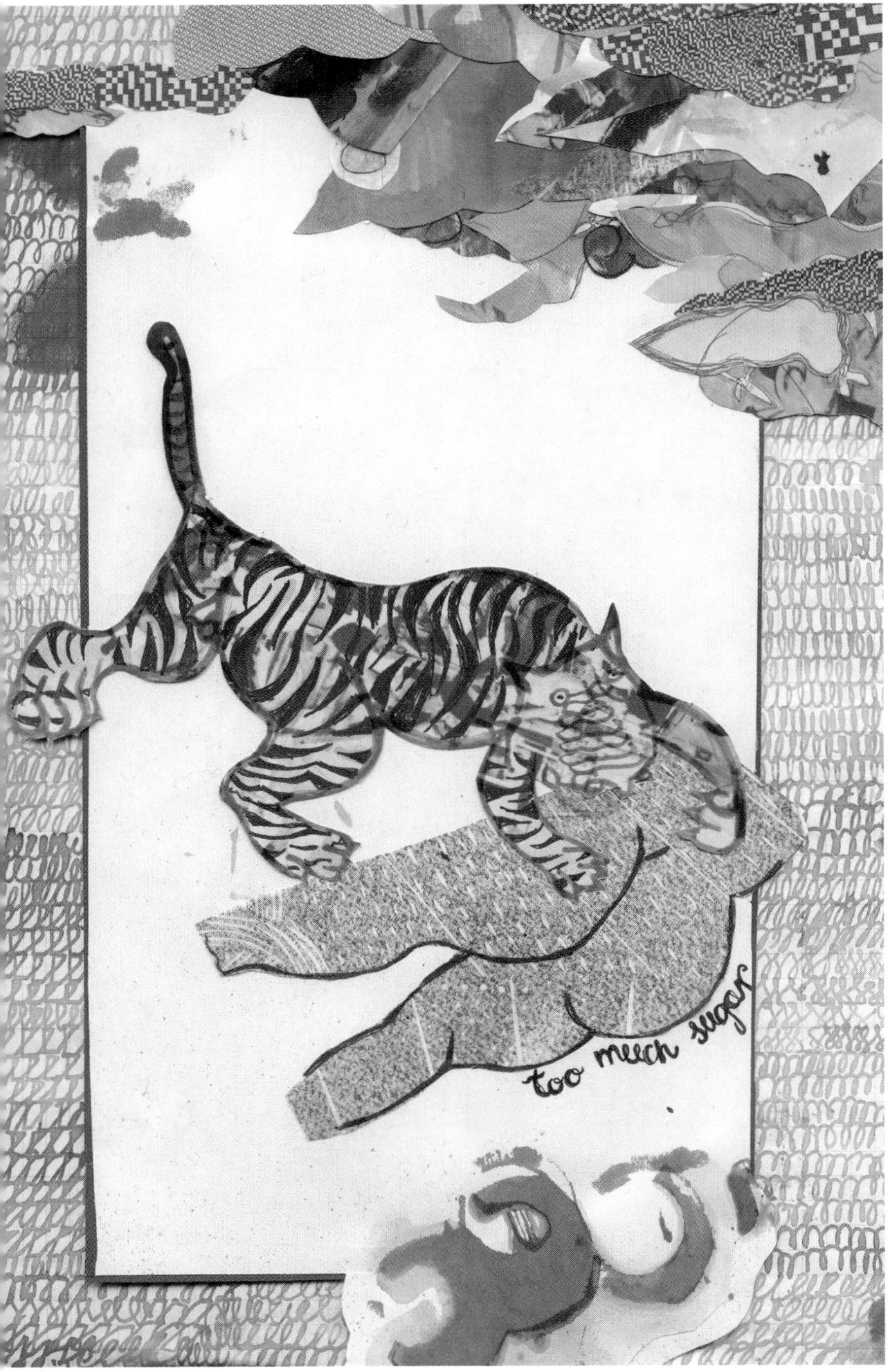
too much sugar

## Larissa Bertonasco

was born in 1972 in Heilbronn. She studied Italian and History Of Art in Siena and Hamburg and Illustration at the Design Department of Armgartstrasse College in Hamburg/ HAW Hamburg. She obtained her diploma in 2003 with her cook book "La nonna La cucina La vita" which became a bestseller and today is in twelfth printing. Since then she is working as a freelance illustrator for magazines, publishing houses and advertising. She hosts culinary readings, exhibitions and since 2004 she is a co-publisher and author of the magazine SPRING by only female graphic artists. She organizes workshops and art projects for children and teenagers, offers courses and gives lectures for students and adults. She is living in Hamburg with her daughter, son and the painter Ari Goldmann.
Her website: http://www.bertonasco.de/

## Christian Maiwald

is a comics activist from Berlin, Germany. He has been working in Comics since 2004 as an editor, producer, moderator and journalist. He is writing about the German comics scene on his website www.dreimalalles.info. Currently he is also putting together a selection of comics from Poland for the June issue of swiss-german magazine STRAPAZIN.

## Małgorzata Rej

In 2009, she graduated from the Faculty of Painting at University of Arts in Poznan, and in 2011 from the Faculty of Graphics and Visual Communications. For 3 years she has been running the Spontaneous Family Manufacture — REJ CAKE — which unites generation by means of flavor. She likes watching other people eating, excursions, and red color. She dislikes stupidity, wasting food and the words "it's impossible". She feels best as a freestyle cook, where ingredients are whatever's left in the fridge.

appetisers

Because nothing is only something ... :)

All my love,
Larisa

**CENTRALA BOOKS**

*Forest Beekeeper and Treasure of Pushcha* by Tomasz Samojlik

*Blacky. Four of Us* by Mateusz Skutnik

*Adventures on a Desret Island* by Maciej Sieńczyk

*Fertility by Mikołaj Pasiński* & Gosia Herba

*Dear Rikard* by Lene Ask

*Tuff Ladies* by Till Lukat

*Moscow* by Øystein Runde & Ida Neverdahl

**WWW.CENTRALA.ORG.UK**